Dr. Math® I

GEOMETRY

. . . .

Learning Geometry Is Easy! Just Ask Dr. Math!

THE MATH FORUM
DREXEL UNIVERSITY

Cartoons by Jessica Wolk-Stanley

JOSSEY-BASS
A Wiley Imprint
www.josseybass.com

Published by Jossey-Bass
A Wiley Imprint
989 Market Street, San Francisco, CA 94103-1741   www.josseybass.com

Published simultaneously in Canada.

Design and production by Navta Associates, Inc.

Jossey-Bass books and products are available through most bookstores. To contact Jossey-Bass directly call our Customer Care Department within the U.S. at 800-956-7739, outside the U.S. at 317-572-3986, or fax 317-572-4002.

Jossey-Bass also publishes its books in a variety of electronic formats. Some content that appears in print may not be available in electronic books.

Library of Congress Cataloging-in-Publication Data

Dr. Math introduces geometry : learning geometry is easy! just ask Dr. Math! / the Math Forum @ Drexel.
    p. cm.
  Includes index.
  ISBN 0-471-22554-1 (pbk. : alk. paper)
1. Geometry—Study and teaching—Juvenile literature. 2.
Geometry—Miscellanea—Juvenile literature. I. Title: Dr. Math introduces geometry. II. Math Forum @ Drexel.
  QA445.D7 2005
  516—dc22   2004002220

FIRST EDITION
PB Printing   10 9 8 7 6 5 4 3 2

To Sarah Seastone (1937–2003),
who loved to play with geometry,
and who gave countless hours to Ask Dr. Math
as editor, archivist, and Math Doctor.

Contents..

Acknowledgments........................

Suzanne Alejandre and Melissa Running created this book based on the work of the Math Doctors, with lots of help from Math Forum employees, past and present:

Annie Fetter, Problem of the Week administrator and geometry consultant

Ian Underwood, Attending Physician

Sarah Seastone, Editor and Archivist

Tom Epp, Archivist

Lynne Steuerle and Frank Wattenberg, contributors to the original plans

Kristina Lasher, Associate Director of Programs

Stephen Weimar, Director of the Math Forum

We are indebted to Jerry Lyons for his valuable advice and encouragement. Our editors at Wiley, Kate Bradford and Kimberly Monroe-Hill, have been of great assistance.

Our heartfelt thanks goes out to the hundreds of Math Doctors who've given so generously of their time and talents over the years, and without whom no one could Ask Dr. Math. We'd especially like to thank those doctors whose work is the basis of this book: Luis Armendariz, Joe Celko, Michael F. Collins, Bob Davies, Tom Davis, Sonya Del Tredici, Concetta Duval, C. Kenneth Fan, Dianna Flaig, Sydney Foster, Sarah Seastone Fought, Margaret Glendis, Chuck Groom, Jerry Jeremiah, Douglas Mar, Elise Fought Oppenheimer, Dave Peterson, Richard Peterson, Paul Roberts, Jodi Schneider, Steven Sinnott, Kate Stange, Jen Taylor, Ian Underwood,

Joe Wallace, Peter Wang, Robert L. Ward, Martin Weissman, John Wilkinson, and Ken Williams.

Drexel University graciously hosts and supports the Math Forum, reflecting its role as a leader in the application of technology to undergraduate and graduate education.

Introduction.......................................

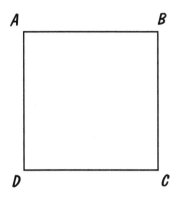

Here's a square. If you tell me its sides measure 2 units long, I can tell you its diagonal (the distance from corner A to C or B to D) is about 2.828. Is it exactly 2.828? No, it's exactly $2\sqrt{2}$. But the diagonal is precisely $2\sqrt{2}$ only if the sides measure *exactly* 2. There isn't a ruler in the world that can measure that precisely—there's some amount of uncertainty in all measurements. Think about this page of your book: Are the corners dog-eared yet? Are they perfectly square even if you look at them under a microscope? Do the sides meet in a perfect right angle? Imagine being able to see the atoms in the paper: do you think they line up exactly? Our rulers aren't fine-grained enough for us to make that kind of measurement, and our world doesn't have neat enough edges.

Maybe you're wondering, then how do we ever build things or make machines that work if we can't measure things precisely? The answer is that we can usually find a way to measure precisely *enough*. If my ruler says a piece of paper is 6 inches long and I fold it in half, I know the result will be about 3 inches. A tape measure will tell a good carpenter enough to make a porch that looks square, even, and level, without the carpenter's knowing its measurements to an accurate hundredth of an inch.

But what if perfect forms existed that we *could* measure precisely? They do in our minds. These are what we study in geometry. Geometry has applications in the physical world, and its principles have made it possible for us to build amazing things from our imperfect materials and measurements.

This book will introduce you to the definitions and properties of two-dimensional objects, including squares, rectangles, and circles. You'll learn how to work with them and how changing one of their dimensions changes other dimensions. You'll also learn about three-dimensional objects: what properties they have in common with two-dimensional forms and what sets them apart. Finally, we'll talk about patterns on surfaces, specifically symmetry and tessellations in two dimensions.

Before you know it, you'll be seeing perfect geometry all around you. Dr. Math welcomes you to the world and language of geometry!

PART 1

Introduction to Two-Dimensional (2-D) Geometric Figures

Two-dimensional geometry, **coordinate plane** geometry, **Cartesian geometry,** and **planar** (pronounced PLANE-er) geometry refer to the same thing: the study of geometric forms in the coordinate plane. Do you remember the coordinate plane? It's a grid system in which two numbers tell you the location of a point—the first, x, tells you how far left or right to go from the **origin** (the center point), and the second number, y, tells you how far up or down to go. The y-axis is **vertical** and the x-axis is **horizontal** (like the horizon).

In elementary school, we talked a lot about shapes and measuring.

True Leon, but I have a feeling we're still going to have plenty of questions to ask Dr. Math.

You'll see a lot more of the coordinate plane in geometry, but sometimes all that matters is knowing that a figure is in the plane or two-dimensional without knowing a precise address for it. This part will introduce you to some of the most common figures in two-dimensional geometry and give you some names for their parts and ways to work with them.

In this part, Dr. Math explains

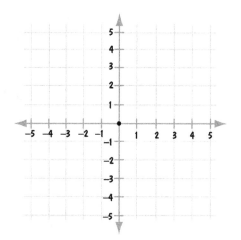

- points, lines, and planes
- angles
- triangles
- quadrilaterals

Points, Lines, and Planes

Points, lines, and planes correspond to talking about no dimensions, one dimension, and two dimensions in the coordinate plane. A line is **one-dimensional,** since one number, the distance from zero, tells you where you are. A **plane** is **two-dimensional,** since you need x and y to locate a point. A **point** is dimensionless. It consists only of location, so it's only possible to be one place if you're on a point—you don't need any extra numbers to tell you where you are. Points, lines, and planes are the foundations of the whole system of geometry.

But point, line, and plane are all **undefined terms.** How can that be? Well, any definition we could give them would depend on the definition of some other mathematical idea that these three terms help define. In other words, the definition would be circular!

Undefined Geometry Terms

Dear Leon,

Your definition would require us to first define "ray" and "direction." Can you do that without reference to "point," "line," and "plane"?

Think of it this way: math is a huge building, in which each part is built by a logical chain of reasoning upon other parts below it. What is the foundation? What is everything else built on?

There must be some lowest level that is not based on anything else; otherwise, the whole thing is circular and never really starts anywhere. The undefined terms are part of that foundation, along with rules that tell us how to prove things are true. The goal of mathematicians has not been to make math entirely self-contained, with no undefined terms, but to minimize the number of definitions so that we have to accept only a few basics, and from there we will discover all of math to be well defined. Also, the goal is to make those terms obvious so that we have no trouble accepting them, even though we can't formally prove their existence.

To put it another way, these terms do have a definition in human terms—that is, we can easily understand what they mean. They simply don't have a mathematical definition in the sense of depending only on other previously defined terms.

—Dr. Math, The Math Forum

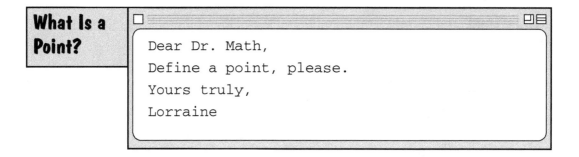

Dear Dr. Math,

Define a point, please.

Yours truly,

Lorraine

Dear Lorraine,

The word "point" is undefined in geometry. But it is pretty easy for us to describe a point, even though it can't be defined. A point is an entity that has only one characteristic: its position. A point has no size, color, smell, or feel. When we talk about points, we are referring to one specific location.

For example, along a number line the number 2 exists at just one point. Points are infinitely small, which means the point at 2 is different from the point at 2.000000001. Here's a picture of a number line:

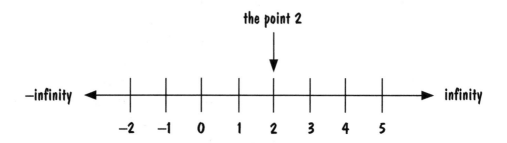

If you want to distinguish one place along a number line, you "point" at it. You label that place with the corresponding number and refer to it with that number.

Now, how do you distinguish a location in two-dimensional space (e.g., a sheet of paper)? Imagine that we have two number lines: one horizontal and the other vertical. We are pointing at a place *p*:

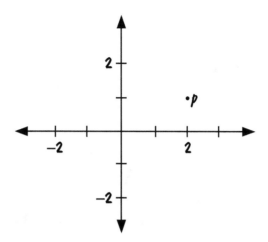

How do we describe where the point *p* is? We can't just say *p* is at 2 because we don't know which number line that refers to. Is it at 2 along the horizontal number line or the vertical one?

To describe where *p* is, you must talk about where it is both horizontally *and* vertically. So, you can say

   p is at 2 horizontally and 1 vertically

However, this is a mouthful. Because describing points in two dimensions is really useful, we have defined some conventions to make life easier. We call the horizontal number line the *x*-axis and the vertical number line the *y*-axis. The convention for talking about points in two dimensions is to write

   (position along *x*-axis, position along *y*-axis)

Therefore,

   p is at (2, 1)

Points in two dimensions can be described by any pair of numbers. For example, (4, 5), (6.23432, 3.14), and (−12, 4) are all points.

—*Dr. Math, The Math Forum*

Dear Dr. Math,

I need to know what a ray, a line segment, and a line are.

Sincerely,

Leon

Dear Leon,

In geometry, you can think of a **line** just like a normal straight line, with a couple of special features. The things that make a line in geometry different from a line in any other context—for example, art class—are that it goes on forever in both directions, it's perfectly straight, and it's not thick.

Mathematicians say that their lines have zero thickness, which is pretty hard to imagine. When we draw lines on paper, they always have at least a little bit of width. But when we study lines in geometry, we think of them as having no width at all.

Here's how a lot of people draw lines on paper. The arrows at the ends mean that the line continues forever in both directions:

Rays and line segments are a lot like lines. A **ray** is like a line, except that it only goes on forever in one direction. So it starts at one point and goes on forever in some direction. You can think of the light coming from the sun as an example of a ray: the starting point is at the sun, and the light goes on forever away from the sun.

Here's how we draw rays:

A **line segment** is a little chunk of a line. It starts at one point, goes for a while, and ends at another point. We draw it like this:

Sometimes we like to attach little dots to represent the endpoints of rays and line segments like this:

—*Dr. Math, The Math Forum*

Later in your geometry career, you'll start seeing a notation for lines and segments that will help you tell them apart. Here's a line:

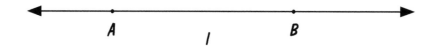

The notation looks like this:

$\overline{AB}$ means the line segment between and including points *A* and *B*; you can also say "segment *AB*."

$\overleftrightarrow{AB}$ means the line indicated by those same points; you can also say "line *AB*."

This line could also be called "line *l*"—lowercase letters are sometimes used for this purpose.

Angles

There are angles all around us—between the hands on a clock, the opening created by a door, even the joints of your body. Any time two lines or line segments or rays intersect, they make **angles.**

What makes one angle different from another? Angles differ in how far open their "jaws" are. If you think of opening an angle starting with two line segments on top of each other, you could open it a little bit, or a pretty big amount, or a whole lot; you could bend it back on itself until the line segments are almost on top of each other again. We often measure angles in degrees to describe how far open the angles are.

In this section, we'll talk about the different kinds of angles and the ways we measure them.

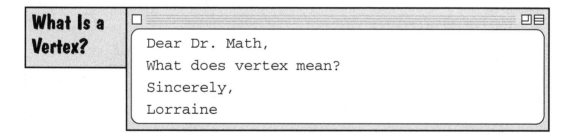

Dear Dr. Math,
What does vertex mean?
Sincerely,
Lorraine

Dear Lorraine,

A **vertex** is the point at which two rays of an angle or two sides of a polygon meet. Vertices (pronounced VER-tih-seez) is the plural of vertex.

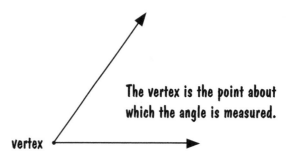

The vertex is the point about which the angle is measured.

vertex

A triangle has three vertices.

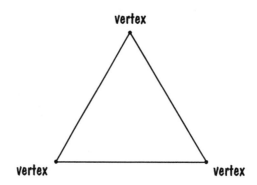

vertex

vertex   vertex

—*Dr. Math, The Math Forum*

Types of Angles: Acute, Right, Obtuse, and Reflex

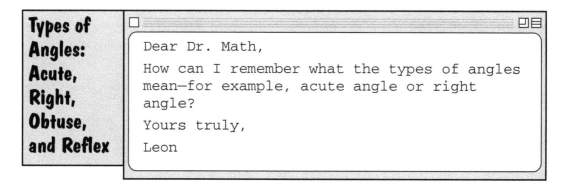

Dear Dr. Math,

How can I remember what the types of angles mean—for example, acute angle or right angle?

Yours truly,

Leon

Dear Leon,

There are three main types of angles. We tell them apart by how big they are. (Angles are often measured in **degrees**; there are 360 degrees in a circle.) Here they are:

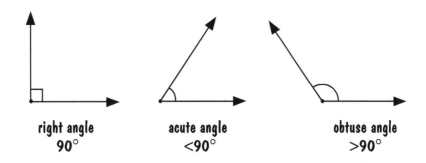

right angle
90°

acute angle
<90°

obtuse angle
>90°

We can start with the right angle: a **right angle** measures exactly 90 degrees. It's called a right angle because it stands upright. Just remember it's an upright angle.

Next is the acute angle. **Acute angles** measure less than 90 degrees. The word "acute" comes from a word that means "sharp." Remember that a sharp pencil or a sharp knife has an acute angle at its point or blade. An acute pain is a sharp pain. Acupuncture uses sharp needles. And, if all else fails, you can remember that an *acute* angle can *cut* you!

Finally, we have the wide-open **obtuse angles,** which measure between 90 and 180 degrees. The word "obtuse" comes from a Latin verb meaning "to make blunt or dull." If a person isn't very sharp (doesn't have an acute intelligence), he may be called obtuse. If that doesn't stick in your mind, just remember that if it isn't right or acute, it's obtuse.

I should mention a fourth kind of angle: the reflex angle. A **reflex angle** is the other side of any other type of angle. Reflex angles measure more than 180 degress. For example, in this diagram, the angle labeled *A* is the reflex angle. (The other angle in the diagram is obtuse.)

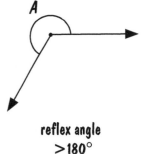

A

reflex angle
>180°

One meaning of reflex is "to bend back"; and the angle kind of looks bent back, like an elbow bent too far. Actually, some people can make a reflex angle with their elbow, and some can't. Can you?

I hope the names are memorable for you now.

—*Dr. Math, The Math Forum*

Complementary and Supplementary Angles

Dear Dr. Math,

In class we're studying complements and supplements of angles. I do not understand any of the terminology behind the problems. Today we took a test, and one of the questions was to find the complement of this angle, c degrees, and I didn't even know where to begin. Another was to find the degrees in the third angle in an isosceles triangle, x degrees, $x - 10$, or something like that. Can you explain this a little better?

Sincerely,

Lorraine

Dear Lorraine,

Part of the problem here is that the names "complement" and "supplement" are kind of confusing, since the literal meanings of these words aren't different enough for us to know which is which, other than by memorizing them.

What are complements and supplements?

If you place two angles next to each other so that they add up to 90 degrees, we say that the angles are **complements.**

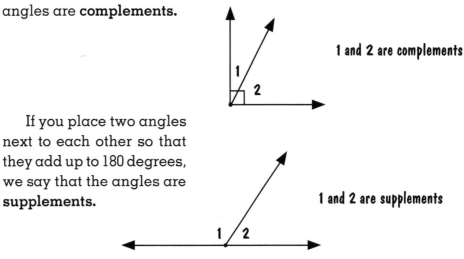

1 and 2 are complements

If you place two angles next to each other so that they add up to 180 degrees, we say that the angles are **supplements.**

1 and 2 are supplements

Here are some examples of complements and supplements:

Complements	Supplements
30 and 60 degrees	30 and 150 degrees
2 and 88 degrees	2 and 178 degrees
14 and 76 degrees	14 and 166 degrees

So what you need to remember is which one adds up to 90 degrees and which one adds up to 180 degrees.

How can you keep them straight? The person who runs the Math Forum's Geometry Problem of the Week tells me that she remembers them this way: c comes before s, and 90 comes before 180. It's the best idea I've heard so far.

If you know that two angles are complements or supplements, you can figure out one given the other. How? Well, if they're supplements, you know that they have to add up to 180:

this + that = 180

So it must be true that

this = 180 − that

and

that = 180 − this

You can do the corresponding calculations for complements using 90 degrees instead of 180 degrees.

So whenever you see the phrase "the supplement of (some angle)°," you can immediately translate it to "180° − (the angle)°." When you have a value for the angle, you end up with something like

the supplement of 26° = (180° − 26°)

which you can just simplify to get a single number. But if you only have a **variable** like x, or an **expression** for the angle, like $x - 10$, then you just have to deal with that by substituting the variable or the expression in the equation. For example:

the supplement of $(x° − 10°) = [180° − (x° − 10°)]$

Note that you have to put the expression in parentheses (or brackets), or you can end up with the wrong thing. In this case,

$[180° − (x° − 10°)]$ is *not* the same as	$(180° − x° − 10°)$	
$(180° − x° + 10°)$	$(180° − 10° − x°)$	
$(190° − x°)$	$(170° − x°)$	

Why should you care about complements and supplements?

Well, in geometry you're constantly dividing things into triangles in order to make them easier to work with. And in every triangle, the measures of the interior angles add up to 180 degrees. So if you know two angles, the third is the supplement of the sum of the other two.

The nicest kind of triangle to work with is a right triangle. In a right triangle, you have one right angle and two other angles. Since they all have to add up to 180 degrees, and since the right angle takes up 90 of those degrees, the other two angles must add up to 90 degrees. So if you know one of the acute angles in a right triangle, the other is just the complement of that angle.

—*Dr. Math, The Math Forum*

ORDER OF OPERATIONS

In case you've forgotten, here's a quick review of the correct order of operations for any expression:

1. Parentheses or brackets

2. Exponents

3. Multiplication and division (left to right)

4. Addition and subtraction (left to right)

For more about this topic, see Section 5, Part 1 of *Dr. Math Gets You Ready for Algebra.*

Alternate and Corresponding Angles

Dear Dr. Math,

Please explain alternate and corresponding angles.

Sincerely,

Leon

Dear Leon,

Let's first look at a diagram that we can refer to when we define corresponding angles and alternate angles:

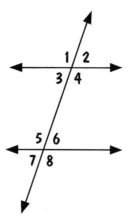

There are a lot of numbers in this diagram! Don't worry, though—we'll figure out what everything means.

Assume that the two horizontal lines are **parallel** (that means they have the same slope and never intersect). The diagonal is called a **transversal,** and as you can see, the intersection of the transversal with the horizontal lines makes lots of different angles. I labeled these angles 1 through 8. Whenever you have a setup like this in which you have two parallel lines and a transversal intersecting them, you can think about corresponding angles and alternate angles.

Look at the diagram. Do you see how we could easily split the angles into two groups? Angles 1, 2, 3, and 4 would be the first group—they are the angles the transversal makes with the higher horizontal line. Angles 5, 6, 7, and 8 would be the second group—they are the angles the transversal makes with the lower horizontal line.

Can you see how the bottom set of four angles looks a lot like the top set of four angles? We say that two angles are **corresponding angles** if they occupy corresponding positions in the two sets of angles. For example, 1 and 5 are corresponding angles because they are both in the top left position: 1 is in the top left corner of the set of angles {1, 2, 3, 4}, while 5 is in the top left corner of the set of angles {5, 6, 7, 8}.

Similarly, 3 and 7 are corresponding angles. There are two more pairs of corresponding angles in the diagram. Can you find them?

One neat and helpful fact about corresponding angles is that they are always equal. Can you see why? (Think about the way the nonparallel line intersects the parallel lines.)

Let's move on to alternate angles.

We say that two angles are **alternate angles** if they fulfill three requirements:

1. They must both be on the **interior** (inside or middle part) of the diagram between the parallel lines, or both on the **exterior** (outside or outer part) of the parallel lines. By interior angles, I mean angles 3, 4, 5, and 6; by exterior angles, I mean angles 1, 2, 7, and 8.

2. They must be on opposite sides of the transversal. Hence 3 and 5 cannot be alternate angles because they are both to the left of the transversal.

3. If two angles are alternate, one must be from the group of angles that has the top horizontal line as one of its sides, and the other angle must be from the group of angles that has the bottom horizontal line as one of its sides. In other words, the last requirement says that a pair of alternate angles must consist of one angle from the set {1, 2, 3, 4} and one angle from the set {5, 6, 7, 8}.

This sounds complicated, but if we look at the diagram and apply the three requirements, it will become clear what we mean by alternate angles.

1. The first requirement tells us that 3, 4, 5, and 6 can only be paired with each other and that 1, 2, 7, and 8 can only be paired with each other. That rules out a lot of possibilities.

2. The second requirement tells us that a pair of alternate angles must be on opposite sides of the transversal. So, 2 and 8 cannot be a pair of alternate angles. Similarly, 4 and 6 cannot be a pair of alternate angles.

3. Applying the final constraint, we see that there are exactly four pairs of alternate angles in the diagram. One pair is 3 and 6. Angles 3 and 6 fulfill all the requirements of alternate angles: they are interior angles, they are on opposite sides of the transversal, and they come from different groups of angles. Can you find the other three pairs of alternate angles?

A helpful fact about alternate angles is that they, too, are equal in measure. This fact can make proofs much easier! Can you see why they are equal?

—Dr. Math, The Math Forum

Alternate Exterior Angles

Dear Dr. Math,

I have been trying to find out what alternate exterior angles are for hours! My teacher assigned us a vocabulary sheet for geometry, and the only term I can't find is alternate exterior angles. I know what an alternate interior angle is but not an exterior one. I am completely clueless. Please help!

Sincerely,

Lorraine

Dear Lorraine,

Here's a clue from everyday English usage: "interior" means "inside," and "exterior" means "outside." (You may see those words on paint can labels, for example.)

So alternate *interior* angles are on opposite sides of the transversal, inside or between the parallel lines, like the pair of angles labeled 1 and the pair labeled 2 here:

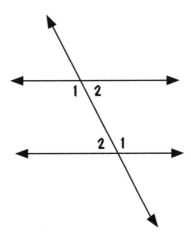

Alternate *exterior* angles are also on opposite sides of the transversal but outside the parallel lines:

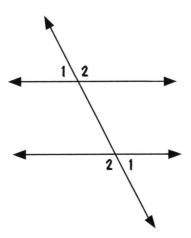

I suspect a lot of students hear these phrases and never stop to think what the individual words (alternate, interior, exterior) mean because they expect math terms to be incomprehensible and unrelated to real life! Sometimes math makes more sense than you realize at first.

—*Dr. Math, The Math Forum*

FINDING MATH DEFINITIONS

Maybe I can help so that you do not have to look for hours for the definition of a math term the next time. To find out what a word means, I would first go to a regular English dictionary; then maybe try one of the dictionary or encyclopedia resources listed in our online FAQ, or search our site (mathforum.org); then go to google.com and enter a phrase such as "alternate exterior angles" to see if there is a definition on the Web. You'll find it!

Vertical Angles

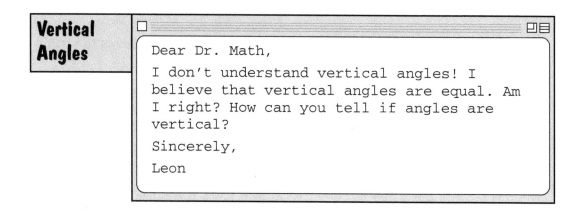

Dear Dr. Math,

I don't understand vertical angles! I believe that vertical angles are equal. Am I right? How can you tell if angles are vertical?

Sincerely,

Leon

Dear Leon,

Get a piece of paper and draw an angle, which we'll call angle 1:

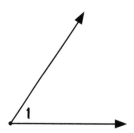

Now take a ruler and extend each ray on the other side of the angle to make two intersecting lines:

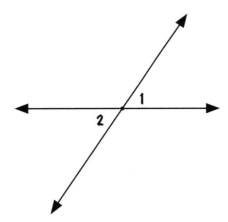

You've just made a new angle 2. The angles 1 and 2 form a pair of vertical angles; they are called **vertical angles** because they are on opposite sides of the same vertex.

Think of the handles and blades of a very simple pair of scissors (with no bend to the handles) as another example. Notice that whatever angle you open the scissors to, the handles will be at the same angle, because vertical angles are always **congruent**—that is, they have the same measure.

The important thing to remember is that not all congruent angles are vertical; angles are vertical because of where they are, not just because they happen to have the same measure. For example, in this diagram, 3 and 4 are congruent but not vertical angles:

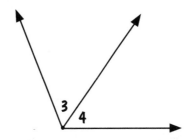

Whenever you see a pair of lines crossing, you will have two pairs of vertical angles. In the diagram below, the vertical angles are 1 and 2, and 3 and 4:

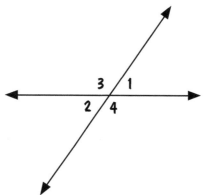

 NAMING ANGLES

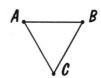

If we wanted to talk about the angles in this diagram, we could call them angles *A*, *B*, and *C*. But if we add a few more objects, it becomes more difficult to tell which angle is identified by any single letter. For example, in this diagram:

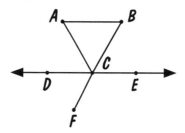

If we referred to angle *C*, which angle would we mean? Mathematicians use an angle symbol, ∠, and three letters to name specific angles in diagrams like this. You'll find ∠*BCE* here:

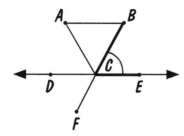

and ∠*ACE* here:

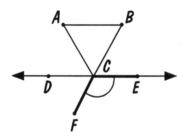

and ∠*FCE* here:

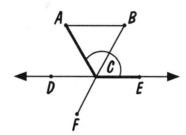

You'll probably see "line *DE*" or "$\overleftrightarrow{DE}$" instead of "∠*DCE*," though. Just keep clear in your mind that there's no bend at *C* in line *DE*!

• •

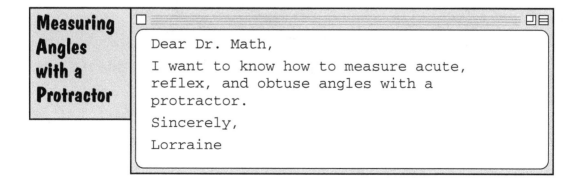

Measuring Angles with a Protractor

Dear Dr. Math,

I want to know how to measure acute, reflex, and obtuse angles with a protractor.

Sincerely,

Lorraine

Dear Lorraine,

As you know, a **protractor** is a tool for measuring angles on paper. The one I'm looking at, which probably looks a lot like yours, looks like this: it's a half-circle of clear plastic, with a line along the straight edge that has a small hole cut out of the middle of it, and a hash mark through the edges of the hole perpendicular to the long line, to help you line up the angle you're measuring. All along the curved edge are little hash marks in degrees, to tell you how big the angle is. On my protractor, there are two sets of numbers: one goes from 0 to 180 clockwise, from left to right, and the other, inner set goes from 0 to 180 counter-clockwise, from right to left. Of course in the middle of the curve where they meet, both sets say 90!

So to measure an acute angle (less than 90 degrees) with this protractor, put the little hole at the vertex of the angle, and align the long line with one of the rays of the angle. Choose the scale that has the zero on the ray of the angle that you lined up with it. Read off the number from this scale at the point where the other side of the angle crosses the protractor. (You may have to use a straightedge to extend this side of the angle if it's not long enough to reach the protractor's marks.)

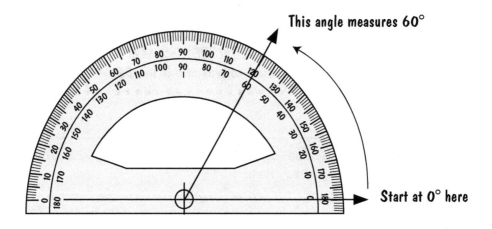

This angle measures 60°

Start at 0° here

Measuring obtuse angles (between 90 and 180 degrees) works exactly the same way.

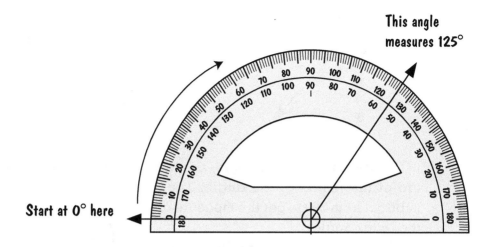

This angle measures 125°

Start at 0° here

Some protractors have only one scale, with zero on both ends and 90 in the middle. If so, then when you measure an obtuse angle, you'll read a number between 0 and 90, then you'll need to subtract that number from 180 to get the measure of the obtuse angle. For instance:

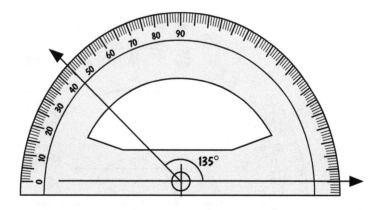

135°

The protractor reads 45 for this angle, but the angle is really

$180° - 45° = 135°$

A reflex angle is the outside of an acute, obtuse, or right angle.

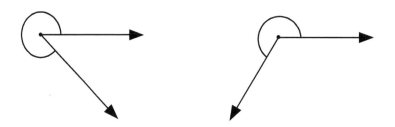

To measure a reflex angle, use the protractor to read the measure of the inside of the angle. Then subtract from 360 to get the measure of the reflex angle.

For example, here is a reflex angle. Note that in this case the other angle is an acute angle:

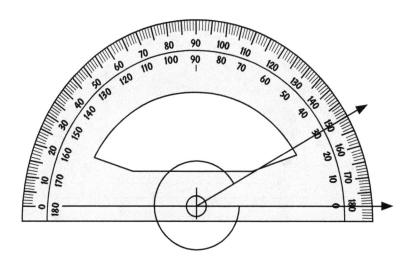

The sum of the two angles is 360 degrees, right? So if we measure the acute angle instead of the reflex angle and subtract its measure from 360 degrees, we'll have the measure of the reflex angle: 360° – 30° = 330°.

—Dr. Math, The Math Forum

Dear Dr. Math,

I would like to know why a circle measures 360 degrees. Is there any special reason for this, or did the Greeks just kind of pick it out? I'm sure there's a rational explanation, but I just can't seem to figure it out. I hate accepting things that I don't understand, and this is something that really bugs me. Please help!

Sincerely,

Leon

Dear Leon,

A circle has 360 degrees, but it also has 400 gradients and approximately 6.2831853 radians. It all depends on what units you measure your angles with.

Allow me to explain. Say you think 360 is a terrible number, and you think that you want a circle to have 100 "somethings" in it. Well, you divide up the circle into 100 equal angles, all coming out from the center, then you call one of these angles a "zink." Then you've just defined a new way to measure a circle. One hundred zinks are in a circle.

This invented unit, the zink, is much like the degree, except the degree is smaller. (Why? Think of how many quarters it takes to make a dollar and how many pennies. Which is bigger?) They are both angle measures, just as the inch and centimeter are both units of length.

The ancient Babylonians (not the Greeks) decided that a circle should contain 360 degrees. In 1 degree there are 60 minutes (that's the same word as the unit of time, but this means one-sixtieth of a degree). Furthermore, in 1 minute there are 60 seconds (again, although they are the same word, this is a unit of measure for angles, not time).

The French in the early days of the metric system, and the British separately around 1900, chose a different way to divide the circle, specifically into 400 gradients. So 1 **gradient** is a tad bit smaller than a degree.

And what's a **radian?** It's a measurement mathematicians use for angles because it's a way to divide the circle into a number of parts that happen to make certain computations easy. The way they decided it was this: They took a circle, say with radius 1 cm. They took a piece of string and made marks on it, evenly spaced 1 cm apart. Then they took the string and wrapped it around the circle. They then asked how many 1-cm pieces of string fit around the circle, and they got the answer of about 6.2831853 pieces. They decided that the angle that a 1-cm piece of string covers as it is wrapped about the edge of a circle of radius 1 cm should be called 1 radian. Weird but true. So there are about 6.2831853 radians in a circle, which means that radians are a lot bigger than degrees. That funny decimal number just happens to be equal to 2 pi, or 2π. We'll talk about pi later in the book. It's a really important number, especially for circles.

Now, you might be wondering why the Babylonians chose the number 360. The reason is that their number system was based on 60. To compare, we base our number system on 10. For us, 10 is a nice, round number, and we find it very convenient to count in multiples of 10. But the Babylonians liked 60.

Why this system was nice for them, nobody knows, but modern mathematicians agree that 60 is a nice number, too, because $60 = 2 \cdot 2 \cdot 3 \cdot 5$ and $360 = 2 \cdot 2 \cdot 2 \cdot 3 \cdot 3 \cdot 5$. What's so neat about that, you ask? Well, you will find that 360 is divisible by 2, 3, 4, 5, 6, 8, 9, 10, 12, 15, 18, and 20. There are few other numbers as small as 360 that have so many different factors. This makes the degree a very nice unit to divide the circle into an equal number of parts: 120 degrees is one third of a circle, 90 degrees is one fourth, and so on.

So while a zink, being $\frac{1}{100}$ of a circle, may seem nice and round to us, it isn't so convenient for dividing a pie into thirds. I mean, whoever heard of asking for a $33\frac{1}{3}$ zink piece of pie?

—*Dr. Math, The Math Forum*

Triangles

Just as there are various kinds of angles, which we discussed in the previous section, there are also various kinds of triangles. In this section, we'll talk about what the differences are and how the Pythagorean theorem can help you find the side lengths of one common type.

Types of Triangles

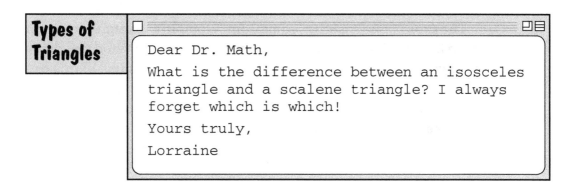

Dear Dr. Math,

What is the difference between an isosceles triangle and a scalene triangle? I always forget which is which!

Yours truly,

Lorraine

Dear Lorraine,

A useful trick in trying to remember these names and many others is to think about the pieces of words that they're made from.

For example, "lateral" always has to do with sides. The fins on the side of a fish are "lateral fins" (as opposed to "dorsal fins," which are on the back). Trade between two countries is "bilateral trade." In football, a "lateral" is when the quarterback tosses the ball to the side instead of throwing it forward, as in a regular pass. And so on.

So "equilateral" means "equal sides," and in fact, all the sides of an **equilateral triangle** are equal. (That means its angles are also the same, and figures with sides and angles all the same are called **regular.**

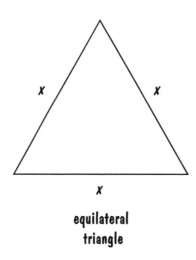

**equilateral
triangle**

The prefix "iso-" means "same." An "isometric" exercise is one in which the position of the muscles stays the same (as when you press your two hands together). Two things that have the same shape are "isomorphic." And so on.

"Sceles" comes from the Greek "skelos," which means "leg." So an **isosceles triangle** is one that has the "same legs" as opposed to "equal sides." In an equilateral triangle, all the sides are the same; but in an isosceles triangle, only two of the sides, called the **legs,** must have the same measure. The other side is called the **base.**

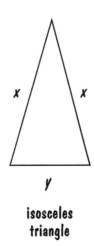

isosceles triangle

"Scalene" comes from the Greek word for "uneven," and a **scalene** triangle is uneven: no side is the same length as any other. But to be honest, usually I just remember that "scalene" means "not equilateral or isosceles."

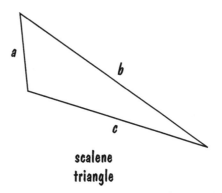

scalene triangle

So what can be learned from this? One lesson is that when you're having trouble remembering a word, it's often a good idea to consult a dictionary to find out the history of the word, because understanding how a word was created can help it seem less random. Another lesson is that many of the words that we find in math and science were made up by people who were familiar with Latin and Greek. So studying word roots, prefixes, and suffixes from these languages can make it much easier to learn mathematical and scientific words!

—*Dr. Math, The Math Forum*

Dear Dr. Math,

What is the Pythagorean theorem?

Yours truly,

Leon

Dear Leon,

Pythagoras was a Greek mathematician who lived around 569–475 B.C. The Babylonians came up with this idea a thousand years earlier, but Pythagoras might have been the first to prove it, so it was named for him. The **Pythagorean theorem** has to do with the lengths of the sides of a right triangle. A right triangle is any triangle that has one right angle (an angle of 90 degrees)—like this:

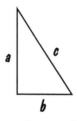

right triangle

If the sides next to the right angle are of lengths a and b, and the third side is of length c, then the Pythagorean theorem says that $a^2 + b^2 = c^2$. That is, $(a \cdot a) + (b \cdot b) = (c \cdot c)$. When people say this, they say, "a squared plus b squared equals c squared":

$$a^2 + b^2 = c^2$$

REMINDER: SQUARES AND SQUARE ROOTS

When you multiply a number by itself, such as $a \cdot a$, you call it "squaring the number," and you write it as a^2. The reverse of that process is called "taking the square root of a number." The square root of a^2 is written $\sqrt{a^2}$ and is equal to a. The square root sign, $\sqrt{}$, is also called a radical.

Some numbers that work in this equation are 3, 4, and 5; and 5, 12, and 13.

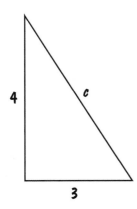

So if you are told that you have a right triangle whose legs are 3 and 4 units, as in this diagram, then you can use this theorem to find out the length of the third side. The third side (the side opposite the right angle in a right triangle) is called the **hypotenuse.**

$$3^2 + 4^2 = 9 + 16$$
$$= 25$$
$$\text{If } c^2 = 25$$
$$c = \sqrt{25}$$

So c = 5.

—*Dr. Math, The Math Forum*

THE PYTHAGOREAN THEOREM

When would I use the Pythagorean theorem?

The Pythagorean theorem is used any time we have a right triangle, we know the length of two sides, and we want to find the third side.

For example, I was in the furniture store the other day and saw a nice entertainment center on sale at a good price. The space for the TV set measured 17×21 inches. I didn't want to take the time to go home to measure my TV set or get the cabinet home only to find that it was too small.

I knew my TV set had a 27-inch screen, and TV screens are measured on the diagonal. To figure out whether my TV would fit, I calculated the diagonal of the TV space in the entertainment center using the Pythagorean theorem:

$$17^2 + 21^2 = 289 + 441$$
$$= 730$$

So the diagonal of the entertainment center is the square root of 730, which is about 27.02 inches.

It seemed like my TV would fit, but the 27-inch diagonal on the TV set measures the screen only, not the housing, speakers, and control buttons. These extend the TV set's diagonal several inches, so I figured that my TV would not fit in the cabinet. When I got home, I measured my TV set and found that the entire set was 21×27.5 inches, so it was a good decision not to buy the entertainment center.

The Pythagorean theorem is also frequently used in more advanced math. The applications that use the Pythagorean theorem include computing the distance between points on a plane; computing perimeters, surface areas, and volumes of various geometric shapes; and calculating the largest and smallest possible perimeters of objects, or surface areas and volumes of various geometric shapes.

Special Right Triangles

Dear Dr. Math,

I need help figuring out something my teacher calls "special right triangles." I've tried to start with a and b, but I get confused. I don't know the next step.

For example, one problem is: find a and b. Simplify radicals whenever possible.

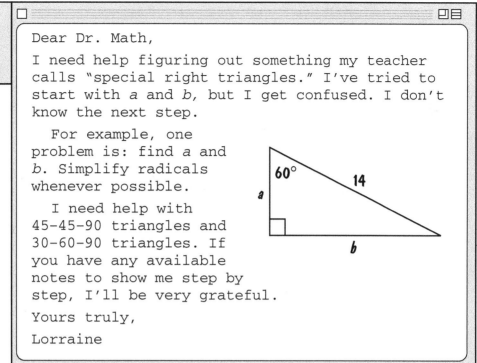

I need help with 45–45–90 triangles and 30–60–90 triangles. If you have any available notes to show me step by step, I'll be very grateful.

Yours truly,

Lorraine

Dear Lorraine,

Thanks for a carefully explained question!

The two special kinds of triangles you describe are special because two sides are related in a simple way. For the 45–45–90 triangle,

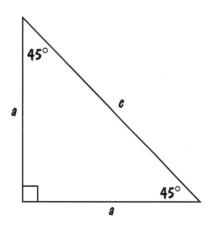

Since the two base angles, the 45-degree angles, are equal, it's an isosceles triangle, and therefore the two sides opposite the 45-degree angles are equal. You can get the length of the other side using the Pythagorean theorem:

$$c^2 = a^2 + a^2$$
$$c = \sqrt{a^2 + a^2}$$
$$= \sqrt{2a^2}$$
$$= a \cdot \sqrt{2}$$

That is, the hypotenuse is the square root of 2 times the length of the other sides.

For the 30–60–90 triangle, the important thing to know is that it's exactly half of an equilateral triangle:

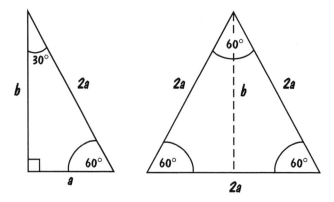

This means that the side opposite the 30-degree angle is half the length of the hypotenuse. Again, you can get the length of the third side by using the Pythagorean theorem:

$$b = \sqrt{(2a)^2 - (a)^2} = \sqrt{4a^2 - a^2} = \sqrt{3a^2} = a \cdot \sqrt{3}$$

So in your first problem, we're dealing with another 30–60–90 triangle, and a must be half of 14, or 7 (just imagine completing the equilateral triangle by reflecting the triangle over side b if this isn't clear). You can use the Pythagorean theorem directly on these numbers, or multiply 7 by the square root of 3 from the formula above to get the answer.

If you prefer, just try memorizing these diagrams:

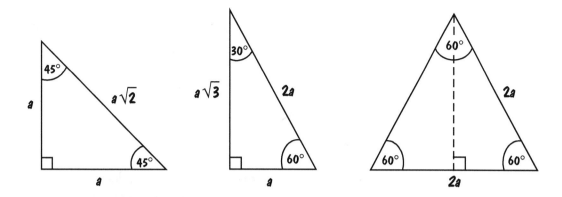

If you have trouble remembering which triangle uses the $\sqrt{3}$ and which uses the $\sqrt{2}$, just remember that the 45–45–90 triangle has two different edge lengths, and it gets the $\sqrt{2}$. The 30–60–90 triangle has three different edge lengths, and it gets the $\sqrt{3}$.

—Dr. Math, The Math Forum

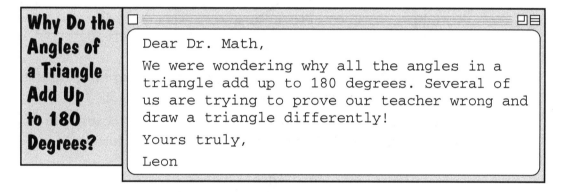

Why Do the Angles of a Triangle Add Up to 180 Degrees?

Dear Dr. Math,

We were wondering why all the angles in a triangle add up to 180 degrees. Several of us are trying to prove our teacher wrong and draw a triangle differently!

Yours truly,

Leon

Dear Leon,

There are several ways that you can show the angles of a triangle add up to 180 degrees. The first example I'll give you involves paper and pencil. The other three examples are more formal in that you construct a figure and use some of the rules of geometry. If you don't understand the last few examples all the way, don't worry about it. You'll cover that stuff in more detail later on.

1. Here's a simple way to demonstrate that the three angles of a triangle add up to 180 degrees: the angles can be put together

to form a straight angle (a line). Make a triangle out of paper, tear off the three corners, and fit them together at the points. They should always form a straight line:

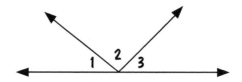

Here's another way to do pretty much the same thing: make a paper triangle in which angles 1 and 3 are both acute (2 may be obtuse) and fold the corners in (dividing two edges in half) so that they all meet on the remaining edge:

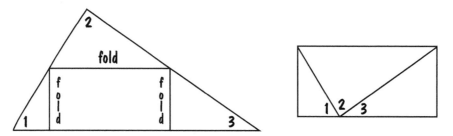

You will end up with a rectangle surrounding three angles that together form its bottom edge: 180 degrees.

2. Let *ABC* be a triangle. Draw a line through C parallel to *AB* (we'll label two points on this line *D* and *E* for clarity):

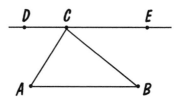

Because line *BC* cuts across two parallel lines, that makes it a transversal. So $\angle BCE = \angle CBA$ and $\angle ACD = \angle CAB$ because they are alternate interior angles. Since $\angle BCE + \angle BCA + \angle ACD = 180°$ (they form a straight angle), the same goes for the angles of triangle *ABC*.

3. Let ABC be a triangle. Let A' be the midpoint of BC, B' the midpoint of AC, and C' the midpoint of AB:

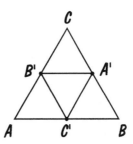

In this way we form four congruent triangles $A'B'C'$, $AB'C'$, $A'BC'$, and $A'B'C$, of which the sum of the angles is equal to the sum of the angles of ABC. If we leave out the angles of triangle ABC, three straight angles are left for the sum of three of the triangles. So each triangle must have a sum equal to one straight angle: 180 degrees.

4. Let ABC be a triangle, and consider the following figure:

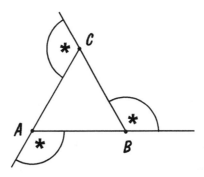

Note that the three angles marked with * add up to one complete turn—that is, 360 degrees. Note also that each of the angles marked with * makes a straight angle when added to one of the angles of ABC. So the three angles marked with * added to the angles of ABC add up to $3 \cdot 180° = 540°$. That leaves $540° - 360° = 180°$ for the angles of ABC.

—*Dr. Math, The Math Forum*

Quadrilaterals

A **polygon** (any figure made up of connected straight line segments) that has four sides is called a **quadrilateral**—remember "lateral" means "side," as in "equilateral," and "quad" means "four." But just knowing something's a quadrilateral doesn't tell you much about its angles or sides except that there are four of them. In this section, we'll discuss the various types of quadrilaterals.

The Seven Quadrilaterals

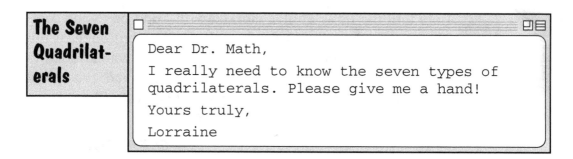

Dear Dr. Math,

I really need to know the seven types of quadrilaterals. Please give me a hand!

Yours truly,

Lorraine

Dear Lorraine,

I think you're talking about these:

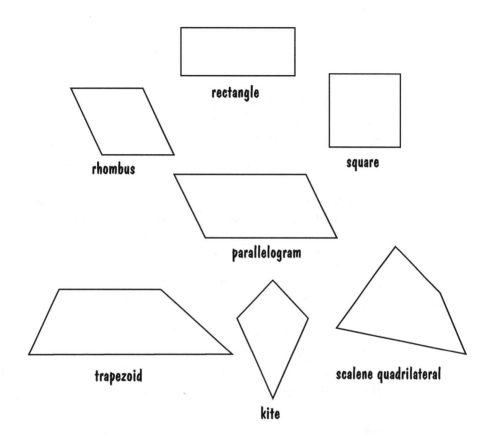

Here are the things you ought to know:

1. A **rhombus** is an equilateral quadrilateral (all sides have the same length).

2. A **rectangle** is an equiangular quadrilateral (all angles have the same measure).

3. A **square** is an equilateral, equiangular quadrilateral, or

simply a regular quadrilateral. Every square is also a rhombus (because it's equilateral) and a rectangle (because it's equiangular).

4. A **parallelogram** is a quadrilateral with exactly two pairs of parallel sides. Every rhombus is a parallelogram and so is every rectangle. And if every rectangle is a parallelogram, then so is every square.

5. There are two definitions commonly used for **trapezoid.** The traditional American definition is a quadrilateral with *exactly* one pair of parallel sides. The British and "new" American definition is a quadrilateral with *at least* one pair of parallel sides. In this book we will use the second definition, which means that all parallelograms (including rhombuses, rectangles, and squares) may be considered trapezoids, because they all have at least one pair of parallel sides. (If the trapezoid is isosceles, then the nonparallel sides have the same length and the base angles are equal.)

6. A **kite** may or may not have parallel sides; it does have two pairs of adjacent sides with equal lengths—that is, instead of being across from each other, the sides with equal lengths are next to each other. So a kite can look like the kind of toy you'd fly in a field on a windy day. But a rhombus and a square are also special cases of a kite: while they do have two pairs of adjacent sides that have equal lengths, those lengths are also equal to each other.

    Just as there are two definitions for the trapezoid, there are two definitions for the kite. We use the one given above; some people use one that says the two pairs of congruent sides must have different lengths, so for them, a rhombus (and therefore a square) is not a kite.

7. A **scalene** quadrilateral has four unequal sides that are not parallel.

—*Dr. Math, The Math Forum*

```
Dear Dr. Math,

I am looking for a diagram that will accu-
rately display the relation among trape-
zoids, parallelograms, kites, rhombuses,
rectangles, and squares. Is a square also a
kite? Is a kite defined as "a quadrilateral
having at least two pairs of adjacent sides
congruent, with no sides used twice in the
pairs"? Why the "at least two pairs" and the
"no sides used twice"?

Yours truly,

Leon
```

Dear Leon,

Your definition of a kite seems awkward. The people who wrote the definition want to make sure you don't count three consecutive congruent sides as two pairs, so they say you can't use the same side twice. I can't imagine why they bother saying "at least two pairs," since once you've chosen two separate pairs, you've used up all the sides. Maybe they want to make sure that they allow for the square, in which there are four pairs of congruent sides, giving two ways to choose two sides that are disjoint to fit the other rule. In any case, the square is a kite by the definition we use. (If you are studying kites in school, check your math book and with your teacher to be sure they both use the same definition, since there's another definition by which the square is not a kite.)

Now for your other question. Here's a diagram showing the relationships between shapes. The lines indicate that the lower term is a subset, or special case, of the upper term. For example, a rectangle is a type of parallelogram *and* a type of isosceles trapezoid, but a rectangle is not a type of rhombus.

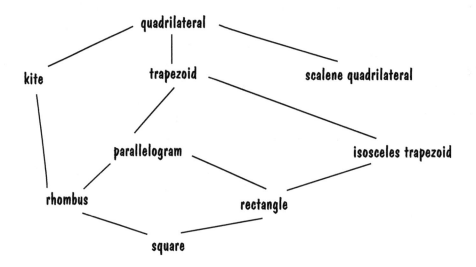

Keep your quadrilateral definitions handy, and check to see if the diagram makes sense to you. Here are some of the things it should tell you. Some quadrilaterals are kites, some are trapezoids, and some are scalene quadrilaterals. Some trapezoids are parallelograms, some are isosceles, and some are neither. Parallelograms that are also isosceles trapezoids are rectangles; those that are both isosceles trapezoids and rhombuses are squares.

Not only are all rectangles parallelograms, but all of the properties of parallelograms are true for rectangles. Two properties of parallelograms are that the opposite sides are parallel and the diagonals bisect each other. Since rectangles and rhombuses are parallelograms, then they also have opposite sides that are parallel and diagonals that bisect each other.

Note that I am using the definition of a trapezoid that says that *at least* one pair of the sides must be parallel. If we have two sides that are parallel, then it's also a parallelogram. Some math books use a different definition in which *exactly* one pair of sides is parallel.

—*Dr. Math, The Math Forum*

Resources on the Web

Learn more about two-dimensional geometric figures at these sites:

Math Forum: Ask Dr. Math: Point and Line

mathforum.org/library/drmath/view/55297.html

A point has no dimension (I'm assuming), and a line, which has dimension, is a bunch of points strung together. How does something without dimension create something with dimension?

Math Forum: Problems of the Week: Middle School: Back Yard Trees

mathforum.org/midpow/solutions/solution.ehtml?puzzle=35

How many different quadrilaterals can be formed by joining any four of the nine trees in my backyard?

Math Forum: Problems of the Week: Middle School: Picture-Perfect Geometry

mathforum.org/midpow/solutions/solution.ehtml?puzzle=97

Graph four points and name the figure that you have drawn.

Math Forum: Problems of the Week: Middle School: Shapes Rock

mathforum.org/midpow/solutions/solution.ehtml?puzzle=93

Find the number of diagonals in a polygon of forty sides.

Math Forum: Sketchpad for Little Ones

mathforum.org/sketchpad/littleones/

A variety of introductory Geometer's Sketchpad activities originally written for second through sixth grades but that older students have also found useful.

Shodor Organization: Project Interactivate: Angles

shodor.org/interactivate/activities/angles/

Students practice their knowledge of acute, obtuse, and alternate angles.

Shodor Organization: Project Interactivate: Triangle Explorer

shodor.org/interactivate/activities/triangle/

Students learn about areas of triangles and about the Cartesian coordinate system through experimenting with triangles drawn on a grid.

Shodor Organization: Project Interactivate: Pythagorean Explorer

shodor.org/interactivate/activities/pyth2/

Students find the length of a side of a right triangle by using the Pythagorean theorem, then check their answers.

Areas and Perimeters of Two-Dimensional (2-D) Geometric Figures

PART 2

In planar, or two-dimensional, geometry, area and perimeter are two of the most common characteristics of shapes that you'll have to work with. **Perimeter** is the distance around a shape, and **area** is the surface that is surrounded by the perimeter. They correspond to the dimensions involved in the figures: perimeter is one-dimensional, and area is two-dimensional. (When you get to three-dimensional geometry, you can talk about volume, which corresponds to the third dimension.)

In this part, Dr. Math explains

- area and perimeter
- units of area
- areas and perimeters of parallelograms and trapezoids

Area and Perimeter

We've talked about some of the basic shapes of geometry; now let's look at some of their properties. Once you know how many sides a shape has, one of the first questions you might ask is: how big is it? There are two very common ways to measure size. One is area: How much space does the shape cover? If the shape were a table, how big would a tablecloth have to be to cover it without any material hanging over the sides? Another measure of size is perimeter: What's the distance around the shape? If the shape were a cake, how long a squirt of icing would it take to outline the top?

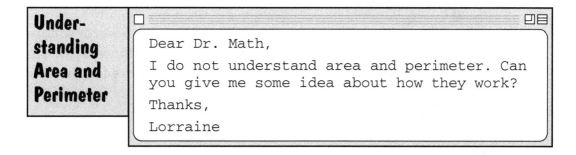
Dear Dr. Math,

I do not understand area and perimeter. Can you give me some idea about how they work?

Thanks,

Lorraine

Dear Lorraine,

The word "perimeter" means "distance around." Think about a rectangle like this one:

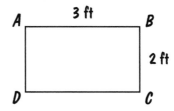

perimeter = 3 + 2 + 3 + 2 = 10 feet

One way to walk around the rectangle would be to move from A to B (a distance of 3 feet), then from B to C (a distance of 2 feet), then from C to D (a distance of 3 feet), and finally from D to A (a distance of 2 feet). The total distance involved would be 3 ft + 2 ft + 3 ft + 2 ft, or 10 ft. So that's the perimeter of the rectangle: 10 feet.

Area is more complicated, because it involves two dimensions, whereas perimeter involves only one. The way I always think of area is in terms of the amount of paint that I would need to cover a shape. If one shape has twice as much area than another shape, I'd need twice as much paint for it.

We use different measurement units for area than for perimeter. We use a linear measure for perimeter—something that measures along a line, like feet or centimeters. For area, we need to measure in two dimensions, so we use square units, like square feet or square centimeters. A square foot is the area of a square whose sides are one foot in length. (A shape that measures one square foot in area may not be shaped like a square, but its area is the same as that of the square.)

For a rectangle, we compute area by multiplying the length by the width:

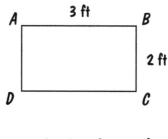

area = 3 · 2 = 6 square feet

One thing it's important to note is that we can have two (or more) rectangles with the same perimeter but different areas:

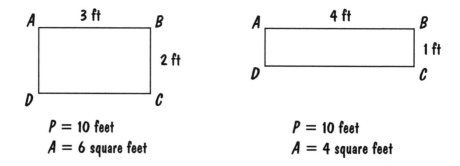

In fact, for a given perimeter, we can make the area as close to zero as we'd like by making the rectangle long and thin:

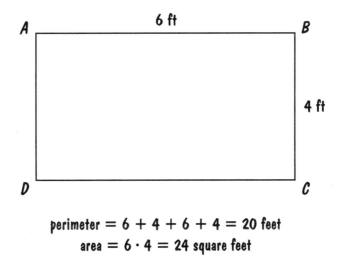

4.9999999 ft

A
D

B
C

0.0000001 ft

$P = 10$ feet

$A = .0000005$ square feet   [Note: drawing not to scale.]

We can make it so long and flat that its height is very close to zero—that makes its area very close to zero, too. You know that somewhere between a long, skinny rectangle and a tall, skinny rectangle there are all sorts of larger areas possible with the same perimeter: a 1×4 rectangle with an area of 5, a 2×3 rectangle with an area of 6, and so on. In fact, it turns out that a square, with the width and height equal, will have the largest area you can make with a given perimeter.

Here's another relation between area and perimeter: if we double the length of each side, we get twice the perimeter but more than twice the area. Let's go back to our 3×2 rectangle for an example. If we doubled its side lengths, here's what we'd get:

A
6 ft
B

4 ft

D
C

perimeter $= 6 + 4 + 6 + 4 = 20$ feet
area $= 6 \cdot 4 = 24$ square feet

Many people get confused about that point, but a diagram can help make things clearer:

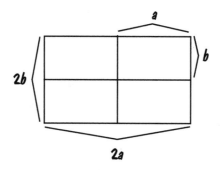

For a rectangle, if I double the length of each side, I get four times the area (but twice the perimeter).

—Dr. Math, The Math Forum

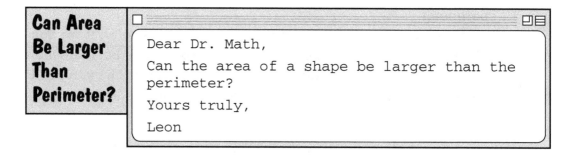

Dear Dr. Math,

Can the area of a shape be larger than the perimeter?

Yours truly,

Leon

Dear Leon,

Strictly speaking, they're not comparable. It's sort of like asking whether a second is larger than an inch. Think about it this way. Suppose I have a square that is 1 foot on each side:

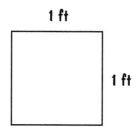

1 ft

1 ft

The area is 1 square foot, and the perimeter is 4 feet. So you'd think that the perimeter is bigger, right?

But here is the same square measured in different units:

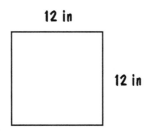

12 in

12 in

Now the area is 144 square inches, and the perimeter is 48 inches. So you'd think that the area is bigger, right?

But you'd think that one is larger or smaller than the other only if you looked at the numbers and ignored the units. When you look at the units, you see that the quantities can't really be compared, so the question of which is bigger doesn't really make sense.

—Dr. Math, The Math Forum

Areas versus Perimeters of Rectangles

Dear Dr. Math,

I don't understand how two rectangles with exactly the same perimeter can enclose different areas. Can you explain that to me?

Yours truly,

Lorraine

Dear Lorraine,

Here's one way to look at it, suggested by a problem someone sent in recently. Let's reverse the question and try to build a rectangle out of twelve 1-inch squares (a fixed area), and we'll see why we won't always get the same perimeter. If you add up the perimeters of each small square, the total will be 48 inches (12 squares multiplied by 4 inches each). If I line up the squares in a row, only two or three sides of each square will be part of the perimeter, while the other sides will be shared with neighbors:

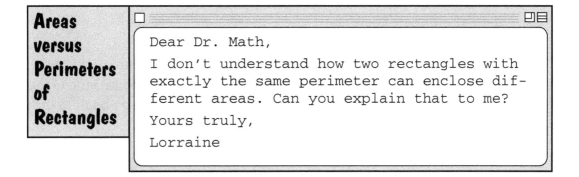

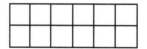

If you count the square edges to find the perimeter, you'll see that it's 26 inches.

Now let's stack the squares closer together, in two rows of six:

Count again: the perimeter is 16 inches.

Now let's lump them even closer together (more squarely), as a 3 × 4 rectangle:

Count again: the perimeter is 14 inches.

Do you see what's happening? The more square the rectangle is, the more edges the squares share, and the less they contribute to the perimeter, so the shorter the perimeter will be. Let's go back to that 1 × 12 rectangle:

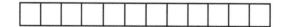

Each of the 11 interior edges between two squares takes away 2 inches from the perimeter (one side of each square), so the perimeter of this rectangle is 48 − 22 = 26 inches. Since the height is 1 and the width is 12, this is correct: 1 + 12 + 1 + 12 = 26 inches.

The 2 × 6 rectangle has 16 interior edges, because more of the squares are touching, so we subtract not 22 but 32 inches from the perimeter, which is 48 − 32 = 16 inches. Yes, this is the same as

2 + 6 + 2 + 6. Likewise the 3×4 rectangle has 17 interior edges, so the perimeter is $48 - 34 = 14$ inches, which is equal to $3 + 4 + 3 + 4$.

The same sort of thing happens with three-dimensional shapes, and this effect is important in such questions as how your body dissipates heat: if we picture the squares as cells, then a flat shape will let each cell be close to the surface and cool itself off, while a rounder shape will force more cells into the interior, where they won't be part of the surface and won't lose heat as easily. Lumpy things have less of an outer surface for the same amount of interior. (That's why elephants have thin ears, to radiate more heat, and why cactuses have thick stems, to retain more moisture.)

Let's look at your problem, which asks the question the other way around: how can the same perimeter enclose different areas? Look at a 1×7 rectangle, still using the little single-unit boxes:

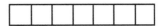

Calculate the area: 7 square inches. Now a 2×6 rectangle, which has the same perimeter as the 1×7 rectangle:

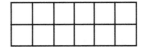

That's got a bigger area: 12 square inches. The number of edges of small squares on the outside of the shape has stayed the same, and the number of small squares actually in the shape has increased.

We could keep going this way, but I think you see that the basic answer to your question is that the area measures the inside of a shape and the perimeter measures the outside, and by changing the dimensions of the shape, it's possible to change both the area and the perimeter. If you keep the area the same and change the dimensions, the perimeter will change. If you keep the perimeter the same and change the dimensions, the area will change.

Thanks for the question. It's fun to think about this sort of thing!

—*Dr. Math, The Math Forum*

Dear Dr. Math,

Does a line have a perimeter? Here's what I'm thinking. In math class we were looking at rectangles with a fixed perimeter of 36 centimeters and a variable area. We were keeping track of the numbers using a chart. I started thinking that for a height of zero, I would need 18 at the base, because that made sense when I looked at the chart. The other kids in my group said that I was wrong because a line of 18 has only a perimeter of 18, and I would need a line of 36 units to get a perimeter of 36 units. Can you help us understand how to think about this?

Yours truly,

Leon

Dear Leon,

I think your group might be confusing length with perimeter. For a line to have perimeter, it would have to have thickness. Lines in geometry have no thickness, so you can only measure along them, not around them.

You can get very close to a thickness of zero with a rectangle, though. If you got very close, the length of the rectangle would be very close to 18. Then to go around such a rectangle, you'd need to walk along a side almost 18 units long, turn a corner and walk almost no units, turn a corner and walk back another nearly 18 units, and turn another corner and finish the last length of nearly zero. That sounds like very close to 36 units in perimeter to me.

—*Dr. Math, The Math Forum*

Dear Dr. Math,

We are reviewing area and perimeter. Our teacher gave us a problem and told us to prove it true or false. I know that the answer is false, but I need help understanding and explaining why it's wrong.

Here is the problem: We have a given square, and we see that if we increase the perimeter, the area increases as well in our new rectangle. Is that always true? Give a thorough explanation and clear examples.

Given square:

P = 12 feet and A = 9 square feet
(In my class, we use P for perimeter and A for area.)

New rectangle:

P = 14 feet and A = 12 square feet

I do see that the theory that as perimeter increases, the area increases as well is not always true, even though it works for the given problem. In my example below, I have a rectangle in which the perimeter increased, but the area decreased, so the theory is wrong (or at least not always right):

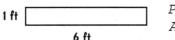

P = 14 feet and
A = 6 square feet

I know how to do the math and figure out perimeter and area, but I don't know how to explain why it doesn't work if one side of the rectangle is 1 foot, and why it did work for the given problem.

Sincerely,

Lorraine

Dear Lorraine,

You are correct that a rectangle with a perimeter greater than 12 (the perimeter of the given square) does not necessarily have an area greater than 9 (the area of the given square). When you are told to disprove a statement, all you need to do is to provide a counterexample—a case that satisfies the givens (a rectangle with a perimeter greater than 12) and does not fit the conclusion (an area greater than 9). You have done this, so you have a thorough explanation with a clear example.

You don't need to explain why the statement is not true in any deeper sense than "because here is an example in which it is not true." But I understand your desire to understand it on a deeper level.

If you have further questions about this, please feel free to ask me. "Why" questions can lead in lots of different directions, and only you can tell me when we have hit on an explanation of the type that will satisfy you. Of course, a true mathematician will never be completely satisfied. There are always more directions to explore.

—Dr. Math, The Math Forum

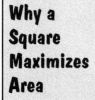

Why a Square Maximizes Area

Dear Dr. Math,

I need to come up with a rectangle with an area greater than 16 square feet and a perimeter of 16 feet.

Sincerely,

Leon

Dear Leon,

Has someone led you to believe that this would be possible? A square with a perimeter of 16 feet has an area of 16 square feet:

Suppose we keep the same perimeter, but use another shape. To do this, we would have to reduce the width by some amount, x, and increase the length by the same amount:

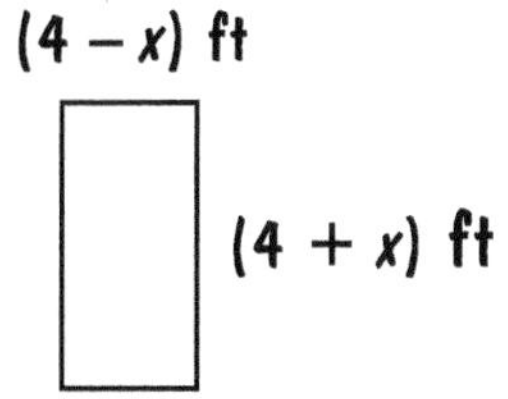

(4 − x) ft

(4 + x) ft

Now the perimeter is still 16 feet, but the area is

$$A = (4 - x)(4 + x)$$
$$= 4^2 - x^2$$
$$= 16 - x^2$$

square feet, which is to say that *any* change we make—from a square to a nonsquare rectangle—will result in a smaller area.

—*Dr. Math, The Math Forum*

Dear Dr. Math,

I have a problem. I have a group of thirteen rectangles arranged into a larger rectangle. I know the area, but I need to find the perimeter. How do I do this? The rectangles are arranged with eleven parallel in one row and two that are sideways on the bottom. The area I'm given is 1,144 square units.

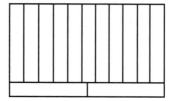

The rectangles are all equal in shape, and I don't know how to find the perimeter.

Sincerely,

Lorraine

Dear Lorraine,

Let's look at a smaller version with three rectangles on top and two on the bottom. All the rectangles are identical in shape, so we can label the diagram with their widths and heights. Can you fill in the rest of the letters in this figure?

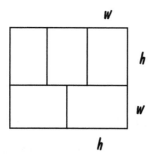

This figure tells us that 3 times the width (w) of a single rectangle is equal to 2 times the height (h) of a single rectangle. Do you see why? We know that the diagram as a whole is a rectangle, so the top and bottom edges are the same length. And the top edge is made up of three w's, and the bottom edge is made up of two h's, meaning that

$$3w = 2h$$

$$\left(\frac{3}{2}\right)w = h$$

What is the area of the whole thing? Again, the figure tells us that the width of the whole thing is $3w$, and the height of the whole thing is $(h + w)$.

Since the area of a rectangle is equal to the width multiplied by the height,

$$\text{area} = 3w(h + w)$$

But we know that $h = \left(\frac{3}{2}\right)w$, so we can substitute that expression for h in our equation for area:

$$\text{area} = 3w\left[\left(\frac{3}{2}\right)w + w\right]$$

$$= 3w\left[\left(\frac{5}{2}\right)w\right]$$

$$= \left(\frac{15}{2}\right)w^2$$

If we use the same idea, wouldn't our equation be $11w = 2h$?

Yes, and then we would have $\left(\frac{11}{2}\right)w = h$, and we can plug in the area and solve for h.

So if I know the area, I can find w by solving the area expression for w; and if I know w, I can find h by using the equation relating h and w.

Can you apply the same reasoning to your problem?

—*Dr. Math, The Math Forum*

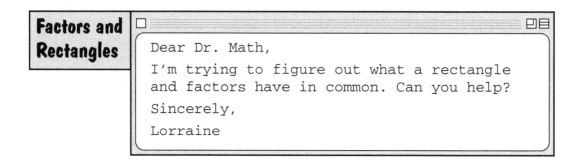

Factors and Rectangles

Dear Dr. Math,
I'm trying to figure out what a rectangle and factors have in common. Can you help?
Sincerely,
Lorraine

Dear Lorraine,

The answer is pretty simple, but it can give you a lot to think about. Since the area of a rectangle is the product of the lengths of the sides, the sides are always factors of the area.

It's easier to picture if you think of building a rectangle out of objects—maybe little square blocks or maybe just arranging squares in a rectangle. If I gave you a handful (or a roomful) of squares and asked you to make a rectangle out of them, you would have to decide what size rectangle you should build. Not all rectangles would work. For example, if you had 14 small squares and tried building a rectangle 5 squares across, you would find that you didn't have enough to make the third row:

That's because 5 is not a factor of 14. If you factor 14, you will find that 14 = 2 · 7 or 1 · 14, so the only rectangles you could make would be 2 × 7 or 7 × 2, or 1 × 14 or 14 × 1.

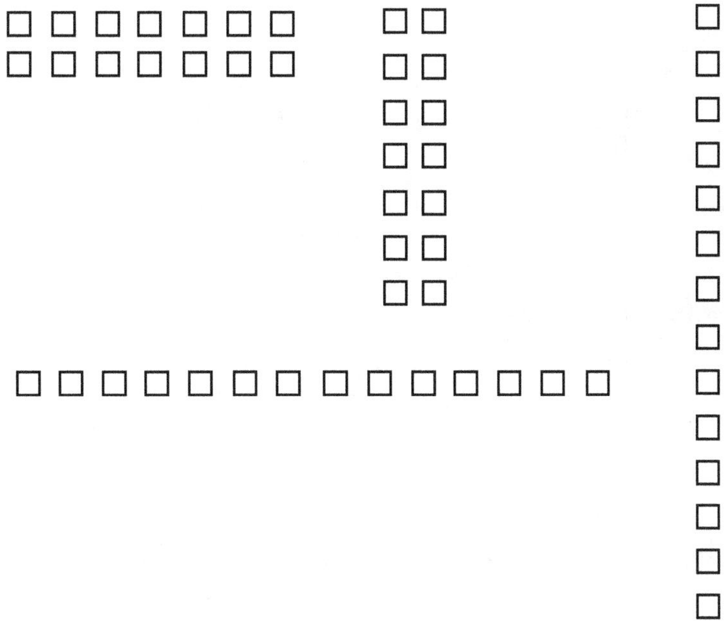

The fun part comes when you have a number that you can factor in more ways. For example, with 36 squares you could make all these rectangles:

1 · 36

2 · 18

3 · 12

4 · 9

6 · 6

9 · 4

12 · 3

18 · 2

36 · 1

Try playing with rectangles for a while. It can really help you get a feel for how multiplication and factoring work!

—*Dr. Math, The Math Forum*

Areas of Triangles versus Areas of Rectangles

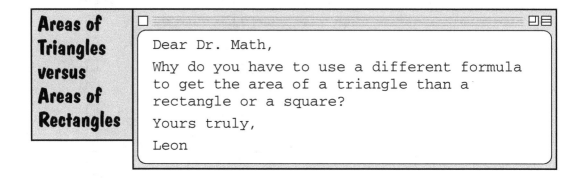

Dear Dr. Math,

Why do you have to use a different formula to get the area of a triangle than a rectangle or a square?

Yours truly,

Leon

Dear Leon,

You use a different formula because it is a different problem. The answer is different, so you need a different process to get the answer. (And you may find that they are not so different after all!)

There is another way to explain this with a diagram. It helps to think of squares and rectangles, because if you think of right triangles in pairs, you can rearrange them to make squares or rectangles. And you already know how to find the area of squares and rectangles.

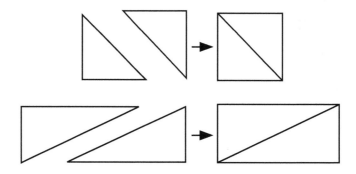

Because two identical right triangles put together along their long sides make a rectangle or a square, that means half the area of the square or rectangle is the area of the triangle. We write this as

$$A = \frac{1}{2} b \cdot h$$

where b is the base and h is the height.

When you are finding the areas of triangles that are not right triangles, try thinking about creating right triangles and applying this same idea. For example:

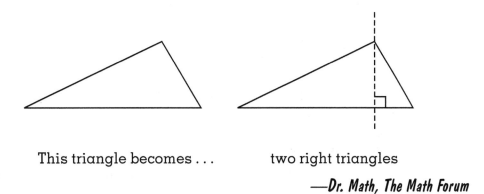

This triangle becomes . . .   two right triangles

—Dr. Math, The Math Forum

Units of Area

When calculating area and perimeter, you're dealing in units of measurement. It's important to keep the units straight in your head while you work with them so that you don't end up with the wrong units at the end of the process. Sometimes they're hard to tell apart. Does 3 square meters mean (3^2)m or 3 m^2? Which area is bigger: pi meters squared or 10,000 pi centimeters squared? This section will help you keep the units straight.

Meters Squared versus Square Meters

Dear Dr. Math,

I'm confused. My friend says that a rectangle 3 meters by 4 meters equals 12 meters squared. I say it is 12 square meters, and that 12 meters squared would be a square measuring 12 meters on each side (or a total of 144 square meters). Who is right?

Yours truly,

Leon

Dear Leon,

It's written as $12\,m^2$ but should be read as "12 square meters" instead of "12 meters squared." As you say, the latter sounds as if it means $(12\,m)^2$, the square of 12 meters, rather than $12(m^2)$, as it really is, 12 times 1 meter squared.

The fact is, however, that you will find both forms used. I think it is generally agreed that "12 square meters" is better, in order to avoid the problem you mentioned, but both are "correct."

—*Dr. Math, The Math Forum*

Notation for Meters Squared and Square Meters

Dear Dr. Math,

If I have a square whose dimensions are 5 m × 5 m, its area is read as 25 square meters. But you state this can also be called 25 meters squared. Isn't 25 meters squared the same as 25 m × 25 m, which is 625 square meters?

How do I write either of these down to avoid confusion?

Sincerely,

Lorraine

Dear Lorraine,

When we say 25 square meters, what we write is

$$25 \text{ m}^2$$

which means

$$25(\text{m}^2)$$

That is, following the conventional order of operations, we evaluate the exponent first, so it applies only to the units. That's different from the square of 25 meters (25 m · 25 m), which would be written as

$$(25 \text{ m})^2 = 25^2 \text{ m}^2$$

and means 25^2, or 625, square meters. Consider the expression

$$5 + 3x^2$$

You don't interpret that last term as $(3x)^2$, right? Same thing here.

To avoid confusion, you have to be careful where you put the exponent. If you put it on the quantity, it means to square the quantity, leaving the units alone. If you put it on the units, it means to square the units, leaving the quantity alone. If you want to square both, you have to use parentheses to extend the scope of the exponent:

$25^2 \text{ m} = (25 \cdot 25)(\text{m})$	$25 \text{ m}^2 = (25)(\text{m} \cdot \text{m})$	$(25 \text{ m})^2 = (25 \cdot 25)(\text{m} \cdot \text{m})$
625 meters, a linear measure	25 square meters, the area of a square 5 m on a side	625 square meters, the area of a square 25 m on a side

—Dr. Math, The Math Forum

Converting to Square Units

Dear Dr. Math,
How do I convert the number 47,224 square miles to kilometers?
Sincerely,
Leon

Dear Leon,

Strictly speaking, you can't. Square miles are a measure of area, and kilometers are a measure of length.

Do you mean how can you convert square miles to square kilometers? Let me show you how to do it with different units, and you can apply the same reasoning to your own problem.

Suppose I have a square that is 2 inches on a side and therefore 4 square inches in area:

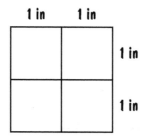

I know that there are 2.54 centimeters in an inch. So I can label my figure this way:

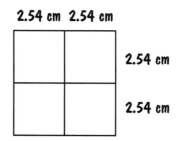

So the area in centimeters is

$$(2.54 + 2.54)(2.54 + 2.54)$$
$$(2 \cdot 2.54)(2 \cdot 2.54)$$

If we look a little more closely, we can see what is going on:

$$4 \text{ in}^2 = (2 \text{ in})(2 \text{ in})$$

The equation for the area of a square.

$$= \left(2 \text{ in} \cdot \frac{2.54 \text{ cm}}{1 \text{ in}} \right)\left(2 \text{ in} \cdot \frac{2.54 \text{ cm}}{1 \text{ in}} \right)$$

Using a conversion factor, there are 2.54 cm in 1 in.

$$= (2 \text{ in})(2 \text{ in})\left(\frac{2.54 \text{ cm}}{1 \text{ in}} \right)\left(\frac{2.54 \text{ cm}}{1 \text{ in}} \right)$$

Multiplication is commutative, so pull everything out of the parentheses and rearrange it.

$$= 4 \text{ in}^2 \left(\frac{2.54 \text{ cm}}{1 \text{ in}} \right)\left(\frac{2.54 \text{ cm}}{1 \text{ in}} \right)$$

Multiply the (2 in)'s.

$$= 4 \text{ in}^2 \cdot \frac{6.4516 \text{ cm}^2}{1 \text{ in}^2}$$

Multiply the other fractions.

$$= 25.8064 \text{ cm}^2$$

The in^2's cancel, so when we multiply, we're left with cm^2 for our units.

So to get the length, I would multiply by a conversion factor. To use a fictional example, let's say I want to convert 21 blinches to ziglofs, and I know that there are 17 blinches for every 35 ziglofs:

$$21 \text{ blinches} \cdot \frac{35 \text{ ziglofs}}{17 \text{ blinches}} = 21 \cdot \frac{35}{17} \text{ ziglofs}$$

But to get the area, I have to multiply by the square of the conversion factor—for example, for the same units:

$$21 \text{ blinches}^2 \left(\frac{35 \text{ ziglofs}}{17 \text{ blinches}} \right)^2 = 21\left(\frac{35}{17} \right)^2 \text{ ziglofs}^2$$

There are 1.609 kilometers in a mile. Can you take it from here?

—*Dr. Math, The Math Forum*

Converting Units

Suppose that you know the speed of a snail in inches/day and that someone wants to know the snail's pace in miles/hour. You can multiply the snail's speed by any fraction that is really 1. For example, 12 inches/1 foot is really just 1 because there are 12 inches in a foot; 60 minutes/1 hour is really just 1 because there are 60 minutes in an hour. So suppose that the snail's pace is 14 inches/day. To convert this to miles/hour, I would multiply by a succession of fractions equivalent to 1:

$$\left(\frac{14 \text{ in}}{1 \text{ day}}\right)\left(\frac{1 \text{ ft}}{12 \text{ in}}\right)\left(\frac{1 \text{ mi}}{5,280 \text{ ft}}\right)\left(\frac{1 \text{ day}}{24 \text{ hr}}\right) = 0.00000921 \text{ mi}/\text{hr}$$

If you write each fraction with a horizontal fraction line, you can see that all the units cancel except the final ones in the answer. In other words, you can cancel units just like you do factors when dealing with fractions.

Areas and Perimeters of Parallelograms and Trapezoids

In the first section, we looked at finding the area and perimeter of squares, rectangles, and triangles. In this section, we'll look at finding the area and perimeter of parallelograms and trapezoids. Do you see from these figures how this section follows from the first one?

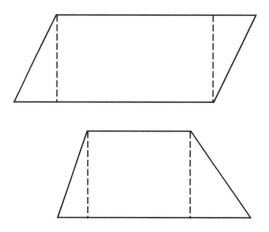

Dear Dr. Math,

I'm a little confused about perimeter and area. I use addition to find the perimeter, and I use multiplication to find the area just the way my teacher taught me. I can do rectangles and squares but not trapezoids, triangles, and other funny-looking shapes. We had to do this problem with a parallelogram that was 27 yards across at the top and bottom, 13 yards at the sides, and 12 yards inside the parallelogram. I came up with 240 yards for the area, but the answer was really 324 yards. Can you help?

Yours truly,

Lorraine

Dear Lorraine,

Perimeter isn't that hard if you remember it is always the sum of the lengths of all the sides of the figure. So in this case, you'd exclude the 12 from your measurements (since it doesn't measure an outside edge of the figure but rather the distance across it), and add 13 twice and 27 twice to get 80 yards for the perimeter.

Area is harder because you have a different formula for each kind of figure. You need to be careful to use the right formula for the figure and to know the meaning of each quantity in the formula.

In your example of the parallelogram, the first mistake you made was using the formula for a trapezoid incorrectly. That formula is

$$\text{area of a trapezoid} = \frac{\text{top} + \text{bottom}}{2} \cdot \text{height}$$

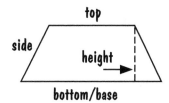

You must be sure that the top and bottom are the lengths of the parallel sides. You can actually use this formula for a parallelogram, because a parallelogram is a special kind of trapezoid with the same length for the top and bottom. But you used length and width (bottom and side) instead of bottom and top.

The formula for a parallelogram is

area of a parallelogram = base · height

This formula works for rectangles and squares, too, because they are special kinds of parallelograms. But you must be careful not to confuse the length of a side with the height. For rectangles and squares, these are the same, but they're different for most parallelograms.

Here is a diagram of your parallelogram:

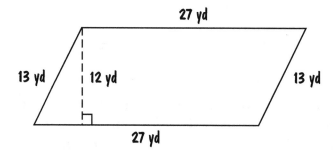

What you should have done is this: The base is 27 yards. I assume that when you say "12 yards inside the parallelogram," you mean the height—the length of a line joining the top and bottom that is **perpendicular** (at right angles) to both of them. Then using the formula

$$\text{area of a parallelogram} = \text{base} \cdot \text{height}$$
$$= 27 \text{ yd} \cdot 12 \text{ yd}$$
$$= 324 \text{ yd}^2$$

Don't forget that area is measured in square units, like square yards (yd^2), not just yards!

So once again, these are the main things to remember:

1. Use the right formula for the figure—know the definitions of parallelogram, trapezoid, and other shapes.

2. Know the definitions of the terms used in the formulas (base, height, etc.) so that you use the right number for each.

And one more thing related to the second item: don't be confused when a figure has more numbers than you need! You didn't need the length of the short side to figure out the area of the parallelogram; that is only needed for the perimeter (unless you're using it to figure out the height, but that's another problem).

—Dr. Math, The Math Forum

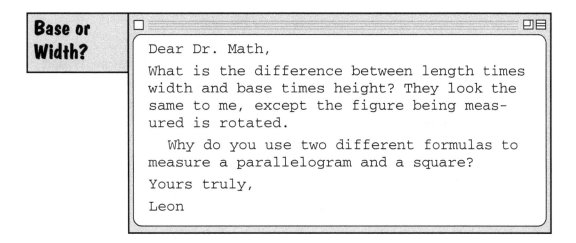

Base or Width?

Dear Dr. Math,

What is the difference between length times width and base times height? They look the same to me, except the figure being measured is rotated.

Why do you use two different formulas to measure a parallelogram and a square?

Yours truly,

Leon

Dear Leon,

These are largely just different terms for the same thing, but they are named differently to remind you of some important details.

We usually use length and width to describe the dimensions of rectangles. (Most of the time, the longer side is *l* and the shorter side is *w*, but it really doesn't matter as long as you're consistent within any single problem.)

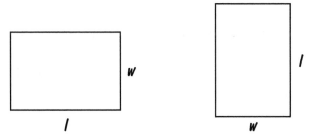

The area is the product of these, whichever way we name them.

Base and height are the terms we usually use for triangles and parallelograms (and trapezoids).

The important thing to remember is that the height is no longer a side of the shape, but the base is:

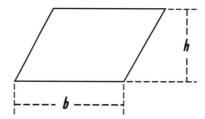

The height is the distance between the top and the bottom, which is measured perpendicular to them. The base is the length of the bottom. If we had said "width," you might think it meant the greatest side-to-side distance, which is not the base:

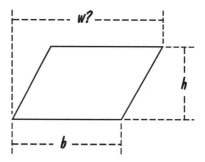

But for a rectangle (which, after all, is a kind of parallelogram), there is no confusion over the meaning of width. It's the same as the base. So you can say that the area is the base times the height or the width times the height.

That's why we use the words we do. Does that help? If you think about it, you will realize that even if you learn only the formula for the parallelogram, you can still find the area of rectangles and squares as well—three for the price of one. Realizing that is a big help!

—*Dr. Math, The Math Forum*

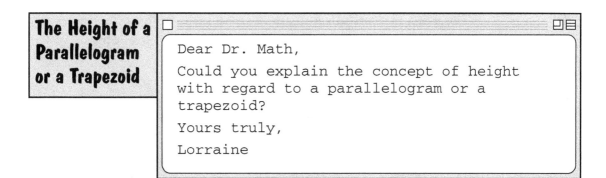

Dear Dr. Math,

Could you explain the concept of height with regard to a parallelogram or a trapezoid?

Yours truly,

Lorraine

Dear Lorraine,

Each of these figures has a pair of parallel sides (the parallelogram has two such pairs). Pick one of these sides and call it the base; then the height is the distance between the line that contains the base and the line that contains the side parallel to it.

The distance between two parallel lines is the length of a line segment with an endpoint on each of the lines that is perpendicular to both lines. Any line in the plane that is perpendicular to one of the lines will be perpendicular to the other, and the length will be the same wherever the segment is located—the distance between parallel lines is constant along their length.

It may be that within the shape you have, no line segment can be drawn perpendicular to the base such that one end lies on the base and the other lies on the parallel side. This is not a problem; we measure the distance between the two *lines*, not the distance between the *segments* of these lines that are the sides of the figure. So you can continue one of the parallel line segments until you have two points that can be connected to make a perpendicular line, like this:

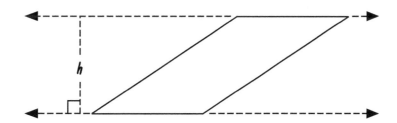

The area of a parallelogram is the length of the base times the height. The area of a trapezoid is the average of the lengths of the base and the side parallel to it times the height:

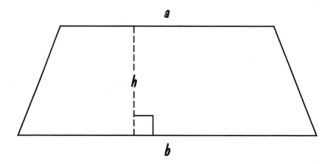

where b is the base, h is the height, and a is the side parallel to the base.

In a parallelogram, you could choose any of the sides and call it the base, as long as you define the height perpendicular to this base; the area will be the same in any case:

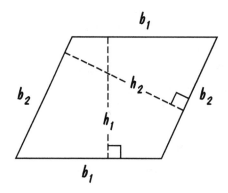

$$area = b_1 \cdot h_1 = b_2 \cdot h_2$$

—Dr. Math, The Math Forum

The Area of a Trapezoid

Dear Dr. Math,

Our math teacher assigned a project, and we have to derive the area of a trapezoid—that is, not simply look up the formula in our math book. Can you help me get started?

Yours truly,

Leon

Dear Leon,

Okay. Draw a trapezoid—any old trapezoid, as long as it isn't a parallelogram. It has two parallel sides of different lengths and two nonparallel sides of different lengths (unless it's an isosceles trapezoid, and then these two sides are the same length). Just so we can talk about this trapezoid, draw the two parallel lines horizontally with the longer side on the bottom.

Now label the upper left corner A, the upper right corner B, the lower right C, and the lower left D. Now we have a trapezoid we can talk about.

In order to find the area of this trapezoid, we have to know a few things:

The length of the line segment AB

The length of the line segment DC

The height of the trapezoid, or the angles of the corners with the lengths of the sides

Look at your trapezoid again, and draw a line from A perpendicular to DC. Call the point where the new line hits DC point E. Then draw another line from B perpendicular to DC, and call that point F. Still with me? You should have a rectangle and two triangles, like this:

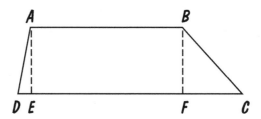

Since we know that *AB* and *DC* are parallel line segments, and we drew *AE* and *BF* perpendicular to *DC*, we know several things:

AB = EF (because *ABEF* is a rectangle).

DAE is a right triangle (because angle *AED* is a right angle).

BCF is a right triangle (because angle *BFC* is a right angle).

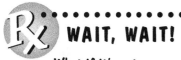

WAIT, WAIT!

What if it's not isosceles?

Just check out the next answer!

So the area of the trapezoid is equal to the area of the rectangle plus the area of each of the triangles.

Let's take a trapezoid where *AB* = 5, *DC* = 9, the height (which is *AE* and *BF*) = 3, and let's say it's an isosceles trapezoid where *AD* = *BC*. You might want to label your trapezoid figure so that you can follow along:

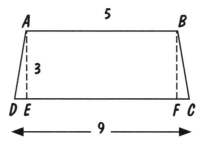

We already know that *AB* = *EF*, because it's a rectangle, so they're both 5. And we know that the height is 3, because that was given. So the area of the rectangle is the base times the height: $5 \cdot 3 = 15$.

Since this is an isosceles trapezoid, we know that the two triangles are exactly the same size and have the same proportions, which means they are congruent triangles. (If you cut two congruent triangles out of the paper, turn them around the right way, and put them on top of each other, they are exactly the same.) So *DE* = *FC*.

Since we know $EF = 5$ (because $AB = 5$) and $DC = 9$, DE and FC both have to be half of $DC - EF$, so we know that DE and FC each have to be 2.

The area of any right triangle is one-half of its base times its height. We know the base is 2 and the height is 3, so the area of one of these triangles is $\frac{1}{2} \cdot 2 \cdot 3 = 3$. And we have two of these triangles, so the total area of this trapezoid is the area of the rectangle plus the areas of the two triangles, or $15 + 3 + 3 = 21$.

If I were going to make a generic formula for an isosceles trapezoid, I'd do it this way:

$$\text{area} = \text{rectangle} + \text{triangle} + \text{triangle}$$

$$\text{area} = \text{base} \cdot \text{height} + \frac{1}{2}\text{base}_1 \cdot \text{height} + \frac{1}{2}\text{base}_2 \cdot \text{height}$$

So, for example:

$$\text{area} = AB \cdot AE + \frac{1}{2}\left[\frac{1}{2}(DC - AB)\right] \cdot AE + \frac{1}{2}\left[\frac{1}{2}(DC - AB)\right] \cdot AE$$

$$\text{area} = AB \cdot AE + \frac{1}{2}(DC - AB) \cdot AE$$

$$\text{area} = AE \cdot \left[AB + \frac{1}{2}(DC - AB)\right]$$

$$\text{area} = AE \cdot \left(AB + \frac{1}{2}DC - \frac{1}{2} \cdot AB\right)$$

$$\text{area} = AE \cdot \left(\frac{1}{2} \cdot AB + \frac{1}{2} \cdot DC\right)$$

$$\text{area} = \frac{1}{2} \cdot AE \cdot (AB + DC)$$

If you check my work here and plug in $AE = 3$, $AB = 5$, and $DC = 9$, do you still get 21?

—*Dr. Math, The Math Forum*

Trapezoids: Visual Proof of the Area Formula

Dear Dr. Math,

We were told that the area of a trapezoid is half the sum of the parallel sides multiplied by the height. How can I visually prove this formula?

I know that with a parallelogram you can cut off the triangle piece at one end, attach it at the other end, and you have a rectangle again, so that proves why the formula *area = base · height* works. Is there a similar way to prove why the trapezoid formula works?

Yours truly,

Lorraine

Dear Lorraine,

Consider this trapezoid, with bases of a and b and a height of h:

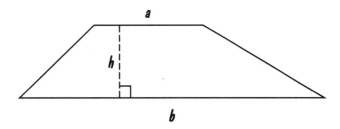

If we connect the midpoints of the legs of the trapezoid, we get a segment that has a length that's exactly between the length of the top (a) and the bottom (b)—it's the average of the other two lengths. So its length is $\frac{a+b}{2}$. We can also construct perpendicular lines from those midpoints to the bottom to construct small right triangles, as in this figure:

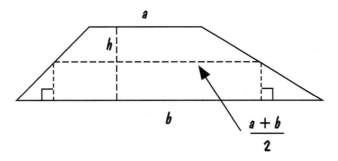

If we rotate those right triangles up around the midpoints until they hit the side of the trapezoid, we end up with a rectangle.

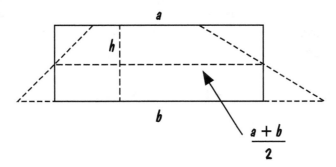

And if you look carefully, you'll see that the length of the rectangle is $\frac{a+b}{2}$ and the height is h, so the area is

$$\text{area of rectangle } = \frac{a+b}{2} \cdot h$$

which is the same as the formula we've learned for the area of a trapezoid.

—Dr. Math, The Math Forum

Resources on the Web

Learn more about area and perimeter at these sites:

Math Forum: An Informal Investigation of Area

mathforum.org/workshops/sum98/participants/muenster/
Step-by-step activity exploring the area of an irregular shape.

Math Forum: The Area of a Parallelogram

mathforum.org/te/exchange/hosted/basden/llgramarea.html
Students learn to calculate the area of a parallelogram.

Math Forum: What Is Area?

mathforum.org/alejandre/frisbie/student.one.inch.tiles.html
Collaborative group activity comparing area and perimeter using Hands-On Math software by Ventura Educational Systems, but the ideas could be adapted to use with other software or a Java applet.

Shodor Organization: Project Interactivate: Area Explorer

shodor.org/interactivate/activities/perm/
Students are shown shapes on a grid after setting the perimeter and are asked to calculate the areas of the shapes.

Shodor Organization: Project Interactivate: Perimeter Explorer

shodor.org/interactivate/activities/permarea/

Students are shown shapes on a grid after setting the area and are asked to calculate the perimeters of the shapes.

Shodor Organization: Project Interactivate: Shape Explorer

shodor.org/interactivate/activities/perimeter/

Students are shown shapes on a grid and are asked to calculate the areas and the perimeters of the shapes.

Shodor Organization: Project Interactivate: Triangle Explorer

shodor.org/interactivate/activities/triangle/

Students learn about the areas of triangles and about the Cartesian coordinate system through experimenting with triangles drawn on a grid.

PART 3

Circles and Pi

Circles get a section all to themselves in this book. That's because circles and polygons have a very important difference: a polygon has multiple straight sides, and a **circle** is a single closed curve. The more sides you have in your polygon, the more you can make it look like a circle, but the sides are still straight. You can't add sides to a circle or take them away without making something that isn't a circle any-

more. We generally use different formulas for measuring circles and polygons, so we'll introduce you to those in this section. You'll need to know about the special number, pi, which we'll also cover here.

In this part, Dr. Math explains

- pi, circle parts, and circle measurements

Pi, Circle Parts, and Circle Measurements

Perhaps the easiest way to understand circles is to construct one. Define any two points, and choose one of them to be the center. The distance between the two points is the **radius.** The circle is made up of *every* point whose distance from the center is equal to the radius. To draw one using a compass, set your compass to the radius you chose. Hold the point of the compass on the center while you move the pencil end around it.

If we choose any two points on a circle, we can connect them with a line segment called a **chord.** If a chord passes through the center of the circle, we give it a special name: **diameter.** A diameter is a type of chord, in the same way that a square is a type of rectangle.

Note that we use the words "radius" and "diameter" in two different ways. A line segment from the center of a circle to any point on the circle is *a* radius of the circle (there are many such segments; they are objects), and the length of such a segment is *the* radius of the circle (there is only one such distance; it is a measurement). Similarly, a chord that passes through the center of a circle is *a* diameter of the circle, and the length of such a chord is *the* diameter of the circle.

We found in an earlier section that two important measurements for polygons are the perimeter and the area. With circles, we still talk

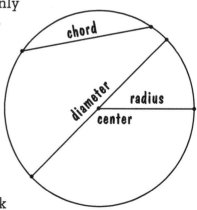

about area, but instead of perimeter, we now talk about circumference. The **circumference** of a circle is the distance around it. As with perimeter, circumference is measured in linear units (inches, feet, etc.). The area of the circle is the number of square units needed to cover its surface. Area is still measured in square units: square inches, square meters, and so on.

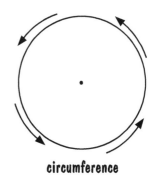

circumference

area

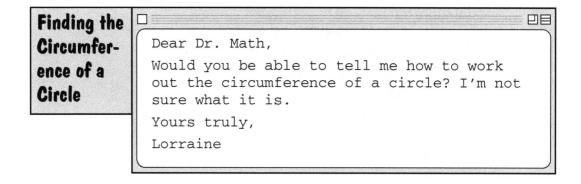

Dear Dr. Math,

Would you be able to tell me how to work out the circumference of a circle? I'm not sure what it is.

Yours truly,

Lorraine

Dear Lorraine,

The circumference of a circle is the distance around it. There is a way to calculate the circumference if you know, or can figure out, another geometric length called the radius.

Here's a diagram of a circle:

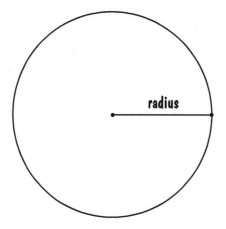

Do you see the dot in the middle of the circle? It's the center of the circle. If you make a line from the center to a point on the circle, that line is going to have the same length no matter what point on the circle you choose. Those special lines are called "radii" (pronounce it as "RAY-dee-eye"). If you're only talking about one of these lines, it is called a "radius." (Notice that there are an infinite number of these radii, but their lengths are the same.)

There is another special line that is associated with the circle, and mathematicians have called it the "diameter." It is simply a line segment from one point on the circle to another point on the circle that also passes through the center of the circle. It looks like this:

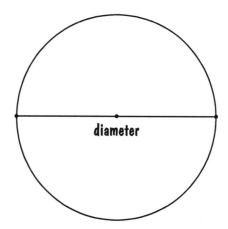

diameter

If you look carefully, you can see that the diameter is one radius from the center to a point on the circle, and another radius from the center to the opposite point on the circle. So the length of the diameter is twice the length of the radius.

Now, what about the circumference? Well, that's just the curved line around the circle. If you cut your circle at one point and straighten it so that it becomes a straight line, the length of that line is going to be the length of the circumference.

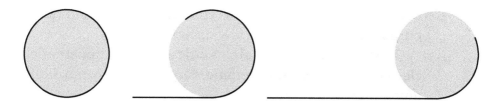

It turns out that circles have a very curious property. If you take the diameter of any circle (no matter what size), the number of diameters that fit in the circumference will be the same for any circle (try to verify it yourself with two pieces of string). Actually the diameter will fit about three times into the circumference but not exactly. There will be a small part of the circumference left.

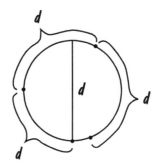

Mathematically speaking, we say that the ratio of the circumference to the diameter is constant (the same number) for all circles. This constant is very famous in mathematics, and it appears, sometimes unexpectedly, in a lot of theorems and equations. Even the Egyptians knew about it thousands of years ago (they said it was 22/7, although we know it's a little less than that). The Greeks also knew about this constant and calculated it to better accuracy using geometrical methods. Mathematicians call this constant **pi** (pronounced "pie"), after the Greek letter π, equivalent to our p.

Pi is a very interesting number that people have studied extensively. It is an irrational number. Essentially, that means we cannot write it as a ratio (we can't get pi by dividing two integers). So we will never know the exact value of pi—we will always be off the true value. We can only get increasingly accurate estimates of what pi is, and people have written programs and found pi to millions of decimal places on the most powerful and fastest computers. (For most purposes, we only need a few decimal places.)

How does all of this help us calculate the circumference of a circle? You know that the circumference divided by the diameter is the number pi for any circle:

$$\pi = \frac{C}{d}$$

or

$$C = \pi \cdot d$$

So if you know the diameter of the circle, you can get the circumference just by multiplying by pi (which is approximately 3.14159 . . .).

Most books give the formula in terms of the radius. Remember that

$$d = 2r$$

so

$$C = \pi(2r)$$
$$= 2\pi r$$

—Dr. Math, The Math Forum

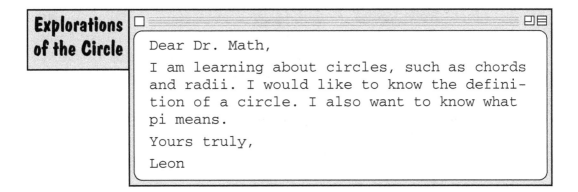

Explorations of the Circle

Dear Dr. Math,

I am learning about circles, such as chords and radii. I would like to know the definition of a circle. I also want to know what pi means.

Yours truly,

Leon

Dear Leon,

You're asking some of the same questions that people have asked for thousands of years. They're very interesting questions. A long time ago, the Greeks wondered what pi was, and a lot of people since then have tried to find out. People have claimed that they've discovered that pi is 22 divided by 7.

Pi is the ratio of the circumference of a circle to its diameter. That is, if you have a string the length of the circumference, pi is how many times it will cover the diameter. It's a little bit more than 3. But pi has all sorts of other strange properties. It's a number that you can never write completely. (That's why we just say "pi" instead of writing it down.) If you start to write pi, it looks like 3.141592653589 . . . , but that's only the beginning of it. It goes on forever.

But what's the definition of a circle? Well, here's one interesting way to think of it: put a thumbtack or a nail in a board and tie a string to it. Tie the other end of the string to a pencil. Now pull the pencil as far away from the nail as you can, and put the point on the board. The string will stop you from pulling too far. Now if you move the pencil while keeping the string pulled tight, you can move it around the nail to draw a circle.

If you think of drawing a circle this way, you will realize that the pencil is always a certain distance from the nail—the distance is the length of the string. So you could say that a circle is made up of all the points that are the same distance from the center point.

If you draw a point on a piece of paper (the center point), then use your ruler to draw other points (whichever ones you like) that are exactly 3 centimeters from the center point, you'll find that you start to get a circle once you've drawn lots of these points. If you could draw enough points, you could fill up this whole circle.

Here's something to try once you've made a circle with a nail and string: try putting two nails in a board or a tabletop, then tie a string in a loop around the two nails. Put your pencil in the string and pull it tight (so that you have a triangle made of two nails and a pencil in a loop of string). Now try moving the pencil while keeping the string tight. What shape did you draw?

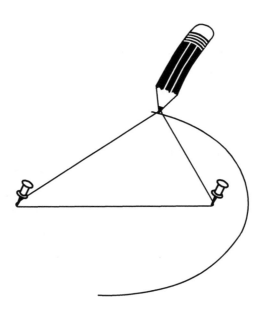

—*Dr. Math, The Math Forum*

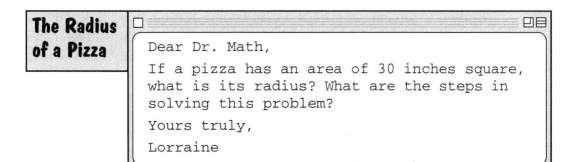

The Radius of a Pizza

Dear Dr. Math,

If a pizza has an area of 30 inches square, what is its radius? What are the steps in solving this problem?

Yours truly,

Lorraine

Dear Lorraine,

Just about the most famous math formula is known as "pie are square," or seriously,

> The area of a circle is pi times the square of the radius length, or $A = \pi r^2$

You know that the area is 30 square inches, so $30 = \pi r^2$. The unknown in this equation is the length r.

Divide both sides of the equation by pi to get $r^2 = \frac{30}{\pi}$, or about 30/3.1416, which is about 9.55. Then r is the square root of this, which comes out to approximately 3.09 inches.

—*Dr. Math, The Math Forum*

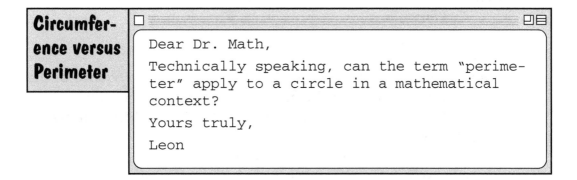

Circumference versus Perimeter

Dear Dr. Math,

Technically speaking, can the term "perimeter" apply to a circle in a mathematical context?

Yours truly,

Leon

Dear Leon,

"Circumference" is just a special term for the perimeter when applied to circles. There is no reason not to allow the word "perimeter" to be applied to circles, as part of a discussion that includes both circles and other shapes. And we're not really sure why one term stuck to the circle and the other term didn't. "Perimeter" comes from Greek words meaning "to measure around," and "circumference" comes from Latin words meaning "to carry around." The Greeks even used the word that became our word "periphery" to mean the perimeter of a circle. In some dictionaries, the definition of circumference is actually "the perimeter of a circle." So perimeter can apply to any figure, but we usually use circumference for circles.

—*Dr. Math, The Math Forum*

Finding the Area of a Circle

Dear Dr. Math,

I haven't figured any of it out, but I want to know how to get the area of a circle. Please help.

Yours truly,

Lorraine

Dear Lorraine,

I'm not sure whether you're asking for the formula for the area of a circle or for an explanation of how it works. I'll give you both.

The formula is

$$A = \pi r^2$$

which means the area is pi (3.14159 . . .) times the square of the radius. To use this formula, measure the radius of the circle (which is half the diameter), square it (multiply it by itself), then multiply the result by π.

There's an interesting way to see why this formula is true, which may help you remember it. (Though the easiest way to remember the formula is the old joke: why do they say "pie are square" when pies are round?)

Picture a circle as a slice of lemon with lots of sections (I'll only show six sections, but you should imagine as many as possible):

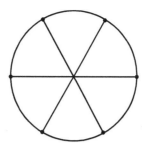

Now cut it along a radius and unroll it:

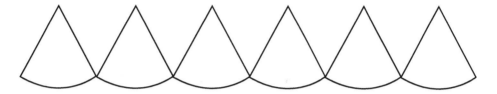

All those sections (technically called sectors of the circle) are close enough to triangles (if you make enough of them) that we can use the triangle formula to figure out their area. Each triangle has an area that can be found using the formula

$$A = \frac{1}{2} b \cdot h$$

Well, what part of the circle makes up the base of the triangles? The circumference, all spread out. What part of the circle makes up the height of each triangle? The radius is the height. That makes our area formula for one triangle

$$A = \frac{1}{2} \left(\frac{1}{6} C \right) \cdot r$$

But wait—there are six triangles, and you have to add them all together to get their total area, right? Well, if you divide the circumference by 6 to get the part that applies to each triangle, then you multiply it by 6 to get the total number of triangles, you're back where you started. So since you know the whole length of the circumference, you can use the formula just once to figure out the area of all six triangles, like this:

$$A = \left[\frac{1}{2} \left(\frac{1}{6} C \right) \cdot r \right] \cdot 6$$

$$= \frac{1}{2} \cdot \frac{1}{6} \cdot C \cdot r \cdot 6$$

$$= \frac{1}{2} \cdot \frac{1}{6} \cdot 6 \cdot C \cdot r$$

$$= \frac{1}{2} \cdot 1 \cdot C \cdot r$$

$$= \frac{1}{2} \cdot C \cdot r$$

You should know that the circumference is pi times the diameter, or

$$C = \pi d = \pi \cdot 2r = 2\pi r$$

so the area is just

$$A = \frac{1}{2} (2\pi r) \cdot r = \pi r^2$$

In other words, the area of a circle is just the area of a triangle whose base is the circumference of the circle and whose height is the radius of the circle.

—*Dr. Math, The Math Forum*

Dear Dr. Math,

I understand that pi is the ratio of a circle's circumference to its diameter. Since pi is irrational, it implies that at the least either the circumference or the diameter must be irrational. I don't understand how that is possible.

  If I had a piece of string 1 inch long and formed it into a circle, couldn't I theoretically measure the diameter of that circle? How could that measurement be irrational? Just because I can't measure it accurately, it doesn't mean that the true length of it is some never-ending decimal.

  If there were some reason that the measurement could never be accurate enough, then perhaps I would understand better. However, I don't see how one length of something can be measured as an exact number and another cannot. There are hypotenuses of right triangles that are rational numbers, so if they can be measured, I don't see why some others cannot, except for the fact that some formula says that they can't.

  In my mind, I know that these lengths are indeed finite, so the decimal must end.

  So that's my question, if you understand it. Thanks.

Yours truly,

Leon

Dear Leon,

Your observation is very smart. Either the circumference or the diameter is not rational. If you have a piece of string exactly 1 inch long and you make it into a perfect circle, the diameter of that circle will be an irrational value. You could try to measure it, but no matter how accurately you did measure it, it would still not be quite accurate enough. So you can never know exactly what the diameter is just by measuring.

If you took that string and made a diameter with it, the circumference would be irrational, and you would never be able to measure the circumference accurately enough. Whatever you measured would be close but not exact.

It's the same problem with a right-angled triangle with short sides exactly 1 inch long:

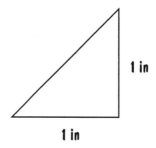

1 in

1 in

The long side is an irrational number. You can't find out what it is by measuring. You can get close, but it's still not exact.

The only way to calculate the exact length of these things is with algebra. Nothing can be measured perfectly accurately. Some things can be measured accurately enough, but that still isn't perfectly accurate.

For example, say we have a piece of string that we've been told is exactly 1 inch long (if you are a centimeter person, then substitute centimeter for inch). We want to measure this piece of string. Our ruler has inches (or centimeters) on it, and when we hold the string up, it looks close to 1, but is it exactly 1 or is it 1.0000000000000000001?

Well, to measure 1.0000000000000000001, we need a ruler with markings that are very close together. But let's say we can measure using a microscope and a very detailed ruler, and we find it isn't 1.000000000000000001. Now the question is whether it is exactly 1 or actually 1.0000000000000000000000000000001—and how are we going to measure that?

See? No matter how accurately we measure, the actual value might not be exactly the value the ruler shows us. That is because rulers don't have an infinite amount of accuracy. No ruler does.

So it doesn't matter if something is exactly 1 or if it is exactly pi, because we can't measure either one of them with enough exactness to be sure. The numbers 1 and pi both have an infinite number of decimal places (it's just that they are all zero in the case of 1), and there is no way to measure to an infinite accuracy.

Any measurement we make is an approximation to the real value. It might be a very good approximation and really, really close, but it will never be exact. That's why algebra was invented. If we can't measure exactly how big something is, then we must calculate the exact size some other way. And that's how we know pi is irrational—not because we measured it and found out it had an infinite number of decimal points, but because algebra says that it must be like that. If we could measure something perfectly, we would find that it is the exact number 1 or the exact number pi, but in reality we can't measure things that accurately.

Let's forget the circle for the moment and look at the hypotenuse of a right triangle or specifically the diagonal of a square.

Length measurements depend on the units by which they're measured. Think of it this way: we measure lengths as ratios of segments, so the length of a side of our square in inches is the ratio of its length to that of a 1-inch segment. So, a given segment might have a rational length or an irrational length, depending on what unit you use to measure it with.

Take that square, for example. If we use the length of a side as our unit, then it is a unit square, and of course its sides have a length of 1. But the diagonal is the square root of 2, which is irrational. If instead we choose to use the diagonal as the unit, then the diagonal would have a rational length, and the sides would be irrational.

So line segments in themselves are not rational or irrational.

Rather, two line segments may be "incommensurable," meaning that the ratio of their lengths is irrational. This idea goes back to the ancient Greeks, who at first assumed that in any figure all the segments would have whole-number lengths (they only knew about whole numbers or at least only trusted those numbers) if they chose a small enough unit. When it was discovered that the diagonal of a square was incommensurable with the side—meaning that it could not be measured as a whole number of the same unit, because the ratio was not a fraction—it ruined a lot of their perfectly good proofs, and they had to start over.

The fact is, the numbers we talk about in math are not something we can ever measure. We can't get enough digits of a decimal to tell whether it is rational; and if we did measure it accurately enough, we would find it is composed of atoms and doesn't have a definite end, anyway. It's only in the ideal world of Euclidean geometry that we can take some segment as our unit and measure everything else exactly enough to know whether it is rational. Irrational numbers are irrelevant to the real world.

—*Dr. Math, The Math Forum*

GREEK PI

Mathematicians chose pi as the letter to represent the number 3.141592 . . . , rather than some other Greek letter like alpha or omega, because it's pi as in perimeter—the letter pi (π) in Greek is like our letter p.

Pi Patterns

Dear Dr. Math,

I'm immensely curious about pi. Does it ever turn into a pattern of zeros and ones, like a computer code?

Yours truly,

Lorraine

Dear Lorraine,

What an interesting question! The answer is that no one knows. Millions and millions of digits of pi have been calculated using supercomputers. The digits look random, with about the same number of zeros and ones and twos and threes and so on spread throughout. Some modern mathematicians suspect that this pattern continues to infinity, which means it will never become a sequence of just ones and zeros or any other digits.

No one really knows, however. The only thing that we know for certain is that pi is irrational: its decimal will not terminate or begin repeating.

If you are interested, you might try to look in some math books in your library. Whole books have been written about pi (a good one is *A History of Pi* by Petr Beckman), and lots of books have chapters about pi, so you might want to start with one of them.

One more thing. I don't know if you have learned about other number systems. Since you are interested in computer codes, perhaps you know that computer scientists like to write numbers in the binary number system, which uses only the digits 1 and 0 to write down every number. For example, the number 13 can be written as 1101 in binary and the fraction $\frac{1}{2}$ can be written as the binary decimal number 0.1.

In binary, everything is written with just ones and zeros. So if pi were written in binary, it would appear to have just ones and zeros also.

—Dr. Math, The Math Forum

BUFFON'S NEEDLE EXPERIMENT

If you throw *n* needles, each of which is length 1, at a floor with horizontal stripes every 1 unit, the ratio of needles that cross a stripe to the total number of needles will approach $2/\pi$ as you have more and more needles. This can be a fun classroom experiment.

esources on the Web

Learn more about circles at these sites:

Math Forum: Designs with Circles—Suzanne Alejandre

mathforum.org/alejandre/circles.html

Students can read about circles in Islamic cultures and explore the geometry involved in circle designs.

Math Forum: The Derivation of Pi

mathforum.org/te/exchange/hosted/basden/pi_3_14159265358.html

Students use real-world objects to understand the concept of a constant such as pi.

Math Forum: Pi Day Songs

mathforum.org/te/exchange/hosted/morehouse/songs.pi.html

Songs to sing as part of a Pi Day celebration.

Math Forum: The Pi Trivia Quiz

mathforum.org/te/exchange/hosted/morehouse/trivia.pi.html

Test your trivia knowledge of pi.

Math Forum: The Area of a Circle

mathforum.org/te/exchange/hosted/basden/circle_area/circle_area.html

Students derive the formula for the area of a circle.

Shodor Organization: Project Interactivate: Buffon's Needle

shodor.org/interactivate/activities/buffon/

This activity allows the user to run a simulation of dropping a needle on a lined sheet of paper and determining the probability of the needle crossing one of the lines.

PART 4

Introduction to Three-Dimensional (3-D) Geometric Figures

We've looked a lot so far at one- and two-dimensional objects. In this part we'll look at three-dimensional objects, or **solids.** Do you remember how it was useful to know something about lines in order to work with polygons and circles? Well, it's useful to know things about polygons and circles in order to work with three-dimensional objects. They're all made using two-dimensional figures, after all: the square can tell you something about the cube, or the square prism; the circle helps you figure out the sphere, the cylinder, and even the cone; the triangle is useful for the tetrahedron and other

I'm sure knowing about squares would be useful for finding things out about cubes.

I hadn't thought about it that way, but that's right – a cube is just six squares stuck together at their edges, after all.

Platonic solids and pyramids. Don't know what Platonic solids are? We'll introduce you to them in this section!

In this part, Dr. Math explains

- polyhedra
- Platonic solids
- surface area
- volume
- nets of solids

Polyhedra

"Polyhedra" is the plural of "polyhedron." The root "poly" is from the Greek word for "many" (which you might remember from "polynomial"). "Hedron" means "face." Compare this with the word "polygon": "gon" is from the Greek word "gonu," which means "angle." So a polygon is a figure with many angles, and a **polyhedron** is a figure with many faces. Knowing where the words come from can help you remember what they mean. In this section, we'll look at the many-faced polyhedra.

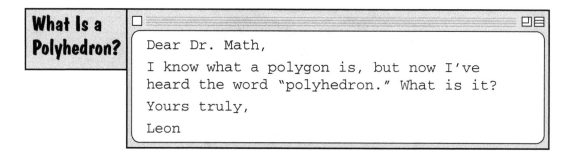

What Is a Polyhedron?

Dear Dr. Math,
I know what a polygon is, but now I've heard the word "polyhedron." What is it?
Yours truly,
Leon

Dear Leon,

The objects you've asked about are solids, not plane figures. The ending "-hedron" tells you that these are **three-dimensional** shapes that have faces rather than sides like a triangle or a square. They have not only length and width but also depth.

The other parts of a polyhedron are called **edges**—where the faces meet—and vertices—corners where angles of the faces coincide (the things that would hurt if you sat on them).

The prefix of each word tells you something about the solid. A cube, for example, has six faces. The other name for the cube is the hexahedron, because the prefix "hexa-" means "six." An icosahedron has twenty triangular faces. The prefix "icosa-" is from the Greek word "eikosi," meaning "twenty."

These two polyhedra (plural of "polyhedron") are special because they are two of the five regular polyhedra, the simplest of which is the tetrahedron. A **regular** polyhedron is a solid having faces (surfaces) in the shape of a regular polygon (all the faces are the same polygon) and the same number of faces meeting at each vertex. The others are the cube (with six square faces, as you know), the octahedron (with eight triangular faces), and the dodecahedron (with twelve faces that are regular pentagons).

When are polyhedra not regular? When their faces are not all alike, or when their faces are alike but not regular. For example, **semiregular polyhedra** are made up of two different types of regular polygons. **Prisms** are a special type of polyhedra that look like you've pressed them from a cookie press or dough squirter: they have two matching faces at opposite ends, and the faces in between are parallelograms formed by connecting the corresponding parts of the matching faces.

—*Dr. Math, The Math Forum*

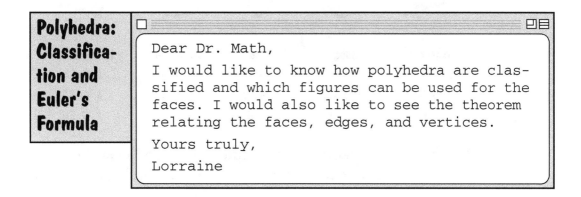

Polyhedra: Classification and Euler's Formula

Dear Dr. Math,

I would like to know how polyhedra are classified and which figures can be used for the faces. I would also like to see the theorem relating the faces, edges, and vertices.

Yours truly,

Lorraine

Dear Lorraine,

The classification of polyhedra is one of the neatest results of early mathematicians. The simplest classification is that of the regular polyhedra. A regular polyhedron has the following three properties:

1. Every face is a regular polygon.
2. Every face is congruent to every other face.
3. Every vertex has the same number of faces around it.

There are five regular polyhedra:

1. The tetrahedron, a triangular pyramid, possesses four vertices, six edges, and four faces.
2. The cube, or hexahedron, which you probably know well, has six faces, twelve edges, and eight vertices.
3. The octahedron has eight triangular faces, twelve edges, and six vertices, and looks like two square-based pyramids connected at their bases.
4. The dodecahedron has twelve pentagonal faces, thirty edges, and twenty vertices.
5. The icosahedron has twenty triangular faces, thirty edges, and twelve vertices.

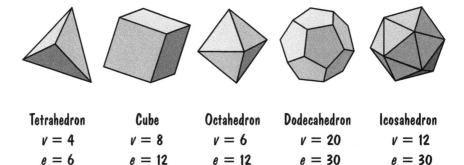

Tetrahedron	Cube	Octahedron	Dodecahedron	Icosahedron
$v = 4$	$v = 8$	$v = 6$	$v = 20$	$v = 12$
$e = 6$	$e = 12$	$e = 12$	$e = 30$	$e = 30$
$f = 4$	$f = 6$	$f = 8$	$f = 12$	$f = 20$

Nonregular polyhedra are also categorized and classified—for example, there are thirteen Archimedean, or semiregular, polyhedra.

These are made of two or more different types of regular polygons, all arranged in the same sequence around each vertex. So you might have a pentagon, a square, a triangle, and a square around each vertex, in that order. There aren't any vertices where the order would be pentagon, triangle, triangle, square.

There is also an interesting relationship among the number of faces (*f*), edges (*e*), and vertices (*v*) of a polyhedron. The mathematician Leonard Euler discovered that in every polyhedron,

$$f - e + v = 2$$

For example, in a cube, $f = 6$, $e = 12$, and $v = 8$, and $6 - 12 + 8 = 2$.

—Dr. Math, The Math Forum

Bases and Faces

Dear Dr. Math,

In math class we are learning about polyhedra, and I can't figure out the difference between a base and a face on the shapes we are learning. What is the difference? How many bases does a cube have, and how many faces does it have?

Yours truly,

Leon

Dear Leon,

What an odd question. We generally use these terms in different settings.

A cube on its own has six faces. Here we're not picturing it set on a table but just sort of floating in space so that all six faces are equal, and we don't think of any of them as special.

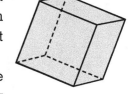

When we are talking about how to calculate the area or the volume, we usually think of one face as the bottom and call it the base, as if we were setting it down on a table to measure it. The top may be seen as the other base, since the two sides are identical, and the other faces are the sides. So when you set the cube down, it has one base (or two if you prefer) and four sides.

It really doesn't make any difference which face you call the base when you talk about a cube, because the faces are all the same. But for, say, a box (a prism like the one below), you have three different lengths (length, width, and height), and by choosing a base, you are deciding which two lengths to use to find the area of the base, and which length to call the height.

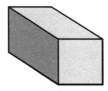

You can choose any face to be the base, and you will get the same answers. Some figures don't have a top: think of a cylinder on its side or a pyramid.

—*Dr. Math, The Math Forum*

Cube Edges

Dear Dr. Math,

How many edges does a cube have? My dad says that there are six edges on a cube, but I think there are twelve edges. I know that a cube has six sides, but edges and sides are not the same.

Yours truly,

Lorraine

Dear Lorraine,

There are eight vertices and six faces on a cube, and there are twelve edges, or lines, connecting one vertex to another. We don't use "side" in relation to cubes, because it can be confusing. (Do we mean the side of a face, which would be an edge, or the side of the whole cube, which might be a face or an edge?). Faces are the two-dimensional squares that make up the cube, edges are where one side of a square meets another along a line, and vertices (plural of the singular vertex) are the places where the corners of the squares meet one another—they're points.

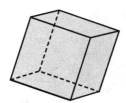

There are eight vertices because you have one square on the bottom and another square above it, and you connect the two squares with edges to form a cube. Since there are four corners on each square and no corners on the edges connecting them, that makes eight vertices. The bottom and top squares both have four edges, so to connect the squares you must add four more, one at each of the corners. This makes twelve edges in total.

The top and bottom squares make two faces, and when you add the four new lines, you add four more faces, for a total of six faces.

It is often hard to see these problems in your mind. Whenever I have trouble visualizing a three-dimensional object, I find that the best thing I can do is grab some clay and make the object so that I can examine it.

So a good way to solve your problem is to find a box (like a shoebox or a cereal box, which is a stretched cube), take a marker pen, and number each of the edges. The beauty of this is that you don't just convince yourself that a box (like a cube) has twelve edges; you can also show this box to your father and convince him, too.

—*Dr. Math, The Math Forum*

Platonic Solids

The Platonic solids are named after Plato, an early Greek mathematician (428–348 B.C.). In his *Timaeus* (a dialogue between Socrates and Critias), there is a mathematical construction of the elements (earth, fire, air, and water), in which the cube, tetrahedron, octahedron, and icosahedron are given as the shapes of the atoms of earth, fire, air, and water. The fifth Platonic solid, the dodecahedron, is Plato's model for the whole universe. Today we still call these shapes the Platonic solids, but we have a new model for the universe and a new understanding of earth, air, fire, and water. You'll need a different book for that information, though!

Dear Dr. Math,

I'm doing some research about Platonic solids. I learned that there are only five Platonic solids. I know that it has something to do with the interior angles, and I did some searches on the Internet, but I could not find a specific solution to the question: why are there only five Platonic solids? If there is a formula, I would like to see that also. Thank you.

Yours truly,

Leon

Dear Leon,

A Platonic solid is one where each face is a regular polygon congruent to every other face, with the same number of faces meeting at each vertex. So we only have to look at one vertex to see what happens at every vertex. At least three faces must meet at each vertex. (Why? Well, think about it. One face not meeting any others is just a flat plane. Two faces meet in a line. Adding a third face to two more faces is what makes a point at their intersection.)

1. Let's start by seeing how many Platonic solids we can make with equilateral triangles. There are three edges per face, and each face is an equilateral triangle with an interior angle of 60 degrees. We can fit three, four, or five of these around a vertex, but we cannot fit six or more and still get a polyhedron. Why? If the number of 60-degree angles together equals 360 degrees, then that would mean that the shape is flat and we would no longer be talking about a solid shape. To find out what that maximum is, think: $360 \div 60 = 6$. This indicates that we cannot fit six or more 60-degree angles around a vertex and still have a polyhedron.

Now think about each case that does work:

a. Three faces meet at each vertex. This is a tetrahedron.

$f = 4, e = 6, v = 4$

$f - e + v = 4 - 6 + 4 = 2$

b. Four faces meet at each vertex. This is an octahedron.

$f = 8, e = 12, v = 6$

$f - e + v = 8 - 12 + 6 = 2$

c. Five faces meet at each vertex. This is an icosahedron.

$f = 20, e = 30, v = 12$

$f - e + v = 20 - 30 + 12 = 2$

2. Let's see how many Platonic solids we can make with squares. There are four edges per face, and each face is a square with an interior angle of 90 degrees. We can fit only three of these around a vertex and still get a solid, not flat, shape, since $360 \div 90 = 4$.

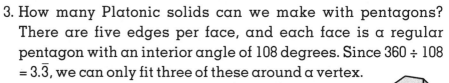

Each vertex touches three faces. This is a cube. $f = 6, e = 12, v = 8.$ $f - e + v = 6 - 12 + 8 = 2.$

3. How many Platonic solids can we make with pentagons? There are five edges per face, and each face is a regular pentagon with an interior angle of 108 degrees. Since $360 \div 108 = 3.\overline{3}$, we can only fit three of these around a vertex.

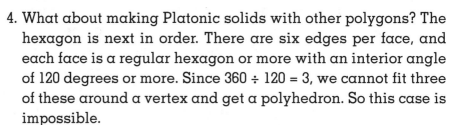

Each vertex touches three faces. This is a dodecahedron. $f = 12, e = 30, v = 20.$ $f - e + v = 12 - 30 + 20 = 2.$

4. What about making Platonic solids with other polygons? The hexagon is next in order. There are six edges per face, and each face is a regular hexagon or more with an interior angle of 120 degrees or more. Since $360 \div 120 = 3$, we cannot fit three of these around a vertex and get a polyhedron. So this case is impossible.

In all, there are just five cases possible.

—*Dr. Math, The Math Forum*

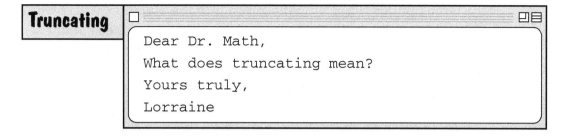

Dear Dr. Math,

What does truncating mean?

Yours truly,

Lorraine

Dear Lorraine,

To truncate a number at the hundredths place would mean to drop the digits to the right of the hundredths place. This is the same as rounding down to the nearest hundredth, unless the number is negative, in which case it is the same as rounding up.

On the other hand, you can truncate a polyhedron by cutting off its corners; a soccer ball is a truncated icosahedron. In general, you can see that the meaning is "to cut off." It is related to the "trunk" of a tree, which is what you get if you cut off the branches.

—Dr. Math, The Math Forum

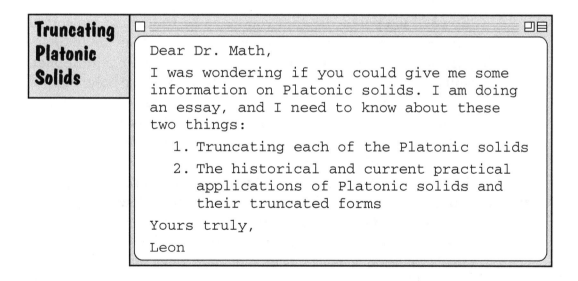

Dear Dr. Math,

I was wondering if you could give me some information on Platonic solids. I am doing an essay, and I need to know about these two things:

1. Truncating each of the Platonic solids
2. The historical and current practical applications of Platonic solids and their truncated forms

Yours truly,

Leon

Dear Leon,

Platonic solids, as you probably know, are the five polyhedra whose faces are all identical regular polygons. They are named for Plato, the Greek philosopher, who theorized that the elements (there were believed to be four of them) were made up of four of these shapes.

Truncation is slicing off the corners (vertices) of a polyhedron. It adds a face at each corner—the cut surface. If three faces meet at a vertex, as in a cube, then the new face is a triangle, with an edge meeting each of the three original faces. What happens to those original faces: How many edges do they have now? How many vertices does the polyhedron have now?

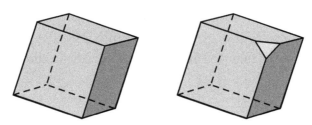

You can truncate just a little or a lot. You can truncate so much that the new faces meet. This will change the number of vertices and the number of edges on the original faces. You can truncate even more. What happens then?

Some of the polyhedra that you make by truncation are sort of regular. Not as regular as the Platonic solids, but they are interesting enough that they are named after another Greek philosopher, Archimedes. The Archimedean solids have regular polygons for faces, but the faces are not all the same. Can you figure out how much to truncate each Platonic solid so that its faces are all regular polygons? For that matter, can you truncate a Platonic solid and end up with another Platonic solid?

You can see that there are a lot of good questions to ask and answer as you explore truncation. Try to make a table. Write down the Platonic solid you start from, how you truncated it (a little? a lot?), and what the resulting solid looks like. Some can be made in more than one way. There are amazing connections among them. Have fun exploring!

As for history and applications, I mentioned Plato and Archimedes. You might look into the ideas that the astronomer Kepler had about these solids. You will recognize one truncated form that is associated with a very popular sport—the soccer ball is made from

a truncated icosahedron. In chemistry, there are polyhedral molecules known as "buckyballs" or "fullerenes" that have gotten a lot of attention lately. These are the same shape as a slightly squashed soccer ball. The man for whom they are named, Buckminster Fuller, also designed a globe or map shaped like a dodecahedron. Those are some things that come to my mind right away.

—*Dr. Math, The Math Forum*

Surface Area

What you learned about two-dimensional figures in Part 1 will be useful in this section, too. When you're working with surface area, you're thinking about the covering or "skin" of each three-dimensional figure. If you could lift the faces off the figures and consider them one at a time, you could see each one as two-dimensional. You can use what you know about calculating the area of a flat figure when you find the surface area of a three-dimensional solid.

Dear Dr. Math,

I don't understand the formulas to figure out the surface area on different kinds of figures. It is really confusing to me, and it's hard to explain what I don't understand.

Yours truly,

Lorraine

Dear Lorraine,

The basic idea is that to find the surface area of a figure, you break the figure up into individual faces, find the area of each face, and add them up. Sometimes this results in a very compact formula that doesn't look very much like what you did, but that's okay, it's still correct.

Let's look at a couple of examples. How about a cube? There are six faces to a cube. (If you forget this, recall that the faces of dice are numbered 1 to 6.)

Each face of a cube is a square, and the length of each side of the square is the same as the length of an edge of the cube. The area of a square is the length of a side multiplied by itself. If we let S stand for surface area, then the surface area of a cube is

S = area of face 1
  + area of face 2
  + area of face 3
  + area of face 4
  + area of face 5
  + area of face 6

S = edge · edge
  + edge · edge
  + edge · edge
  + edge · edge

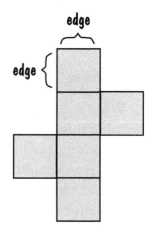

$$+ \text{edge} \cdot \text{edge}$$
$$+ \text{edge} \cdot \text{edge}$$

$$S = 6 \cdot \text{edge} \cdot \text{edge}$$
$$= 6 \cdot \text{edge}^2$$

(The figure above is called a net of the cube: it's what you get if you cut apart some of the faces of the cube and unfold it.)

Now, suppose we don't have a cube but a rectangular prism (like the shape of a cereal box). We still have six faces, but now they come in pairs, and each face is a rectangle. Two of the rectangles have dimensions width by height, two have dimensions width by length, and the remaining two have dimensions length by height. So the surface area is

$$S = \text{area of face 1}$$
$$+ \text{area of face 2}$$
$$+ \text{area of face 3}$$
$$+ \text{area of face 4}$$
$$+ \text{area of face 5}$$
$$+ \text{area of face 6}$$

$$S = \text{width} \cdot \text{height}$$
$$+ \text{width} \cdot \text{height}$$
$$+ \text{width} \cdot \text{length}$$
$$+ \text{width} \cdot \text{length}$$
$$+ \text{length} \cdot \text{height}$$
$$+ \text{length} \cdot \text{height}$$

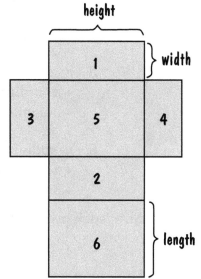

$$S = 2(\text{width} \cdot \text{height} + \text{width} \cdot \text{length} + \text{length} \cdot \text{height})$$

Let's look at one more example: a cylinder. There are three faces to a cylinder: a circular one at each end and the big curved side, which can be pictured rolled out flat as a rectangle.

The area of each circle is pi times the square of the radius. So the surface area is

S = area of circle 1
  + area of circle 2
  + area of side

$S = \pi \cdot \text{radius}^2$
  $+ \pi \cdot \text{radius}^2$
  $+$ area of side

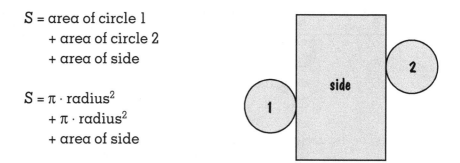

The height of the rectangle (its height is sideways in this illustration, remember) is the height of the whole cylinder. What is the width of the rectangle? It's the circumference of the circles! So we can complete the formula:

$S = \pi \cdot \text{radius}^2$
  $+ \pi \cdot \text{radius}^2$
  $+ \text{height} \cdot \text{circumference}$

$S = \pi \cdot \text{radius}^2$
  $+ \pi \cdot \text{radius}^2$
  $+ \text{height} \cdot \pi \cdot \text{diameter}$

$S = \pi \cdot \text{radius}^2$
  $+ \pi \cdot \text{radius}^2$
  $+ \text{height} \cdot \pi \cdot 2 \cdot \text{radius}$

Now, each of these terms has pi in it, so we can factor that out:

$S = \pi \cdot (\text{radius}^2 + \text{radius}^2 + \text{height} \cdot 2 \cdot \text{radius})$

Each term in parentheses also has a radius in it, so we can factor that out, too:

$S = \pi \cdot \text{radius} \cdot (\text{radius} + \text{radius} + 2 \cdot \text{height})$

We can add the radii together:

$S = \pi \cdot \text{radius} \cdot (2 \cdot \text{radius} + 2 \cdot \text{height})$

And now we can factor out the 2:

$S = 2 \cdot \pi \cdot \text{radius} \cdot (\text{radius} + \text{height})$

Now, here's the thing. If you're not going to use this formula every day, there's absolutely no point in memorizing it. I certainly haven't! If I want to compute the surface area of a cylinder, I'll break it into two circles and a rectangle made from the curved side, compute those areas, and add them up. And I recommend that you do the same thing, rather than trying to learn all the compact formulas.

—Dr. Math, The Math Forum

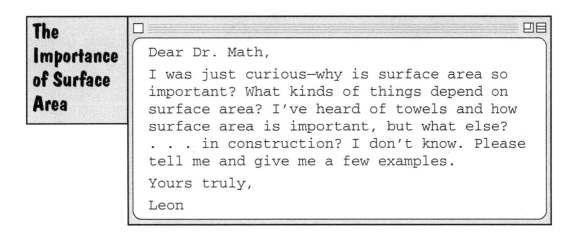

The Importance of Surface Area

Dear Dr. Math,

I was just curious—why is surface area so important? What kinds of things depend on surface area? I've heard of towels and how surface area is important, but what else? . . . in construction? I don't know. Please tell me and give me a few examples.

Yours truly,

Leon

Dear Leon,

In construction, surface area affects planning (how much to buy) and costs (how much to charge) in connection with such things as wallboard, shingles, and paint. In manufacturing, you will have the same issues—say, the cost of making boxes or printing or sheet metal parts. In designing, surface area enters into calculations of wind resistance and drag in cars or airplanes, as well as pressure and strength of materials.

The surface area exposed to air affects how fast something cools or heats or dries out. Elephants, for example, need big ears to increase their surface area for cooling purposes. Many objects have complex shapes to increase their surface area: the inside of your lungs, intestines, and brain; air cleaners; radiators—and towels, as you mentioned, which have greater surface area because of the loops of thread that stick out from them. Other things avoid flat shapes to minimize surface area and keep from drying out: pine needles and cactus plants, for example, or terrariums, which are nearly spherical in order to keep their interiors as moist as possible.

Many things you buy for home use, such as fabric, plastic wrap, and so on, are priced by surface area—or, if not, it will help you to know the cost per amount of surface area to decide which is the best buy.

—*Dr. Math, The Math Forum*

Hah, that's great. What do elephant ears, our Lungs, and our towels have in common? They're all designed to maximize surface area!

Yeah, my mom was telling me why her favorite coffee mug is almost spherical—

It holds heat better that way because it minimizes surface area. A cylinder-shaped mug wouldn't hold heat as well, and a wide, flat bowl-shaped mug would cool off really fast.

Volume

A simple way to think about volume is this: if you have two identical lumps of clay and you make two different shapes with them, the two shapes have the same volume. If you go into a store that sells kitchen supplies and look at measuring cups, you can find them in lots of different shapes: round, square, short, tall, fat, thin. But if two measuring cups are marked with the same measurement—say, one-third cup—then they can hold the same volume, because it takes the same amount of stuff to fill them. That is, you can fill one with water, and if you pour the water into the other cup, it will fill that one, too.

Dear Dr. Math,

What are the definitions of surface area and volume? How do you find the surface area and volume of a rectangular prism and a cube? Can you show me a diagram of a rectangular prism and a cube? What are the differences between surface area and volume? Are there similarities?

Yours truly,

Lorraine

Dear Lorraine,

Let's start out with some general ideas about area and volume, then we'll look at prisms a bit. A mathematician can get very picky about definitions, and sometimes the harder we think, the harder it gets to really define something. But I bet what you probably want is just to understand what we mean when we talk about area and volume.

Basically, the **surface area** of an object means how much paper it would take to cover it (or how much paint, if you follow the directions and don't put it on too thick or too thin). The **volume** is how much clay it would take to make the object, or how much water it would take to fill it (if it were hollow). We measure area in "square somethings," such as square inches. If I cut a piece of paper into 1-inch squares and try to paste them on the surface, how many will it take? Volume is measured in "cubic somethings," such as cubic inches. If I try to build the shape out of 1-inch cubes, how many will it take?

The main similarity between surface area and volume is that both are measurements of the size of something. The main difference is that area deals only with the outside, while volume deals with the whole thing. Area is two-dimensional (like a sheet of paper, which doesn't have any significant thickness), and volume is three-dimensional (it involves the height, width, and thickness of an object). But when you're talking about surface area, you have to be careful, because although the object you're measuring has three dimensions, you're just measuring its surface, which is two-dimensional.

Here's a figure of a rectangular prism:

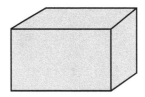

A cube is just a particular kind of rectangular prism that is the same size in all three directions. A rectangular prism can be thought of as the shape you'd get if you put a rectangle flat on the table in front of you, then lifted it straight up and imagined that it left a shape behind. Or you could think of it as a stack of identical rectangles:

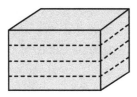

To find the volume, just multiply the three dimensions together. For example, if you have a 2-inch by 3-inch by 4-inch prism, the volume is 2 · 3 · 4 = 24 cubic inches. To see why, just imagine building the prism out of 1-inch cubes. You'll need six (2 · 3) on the bottom layer, six on the next, and so on for four layers, so it will take 6 · 4 = 24 cubes.

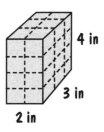

4 in

3 in

2 in

But if you want to calculate the surface area, you have to figure out the area of each rectangular surface. There is a top and a bottom, both $2 \cdot 3$ (6 square inches each), a front and a back, both $2 \cdot 4$ (8 square inches each), and a left and a right side, both $3 \cdot 4$ (12 square inches each), for a total of

$$12 + 16 + 24 = 52 \text{ square inches}$$

Can you picture that? If not, get out some blocks and some paper and do it!

If you like formulas, then for a prism that measures l units long by w units wide by h units tall, the volume is

$$l \cdot w \cdot h$$

and the surface area is

$$2 \cdot l \cdot w + 2 \cdot l \cdot h + 2 \cdot w \cdot h$$

—Dr. Math, The Math Forum

Cups and Volume

Dear Dr. Math,

How can I calculate the volume of a box if I know how many cups of rice (or something like that) fill it?

I don't understand how 2 cups is a volume measure, since volume = length · width · height. For example, if I calculate the box to have a volume of 24 cubic inches, how is that the same as the 2 cups of rice it holds?

Yours truly,

Leon

Dear Leon,

A cup is a unit of volume, just like a cubic inch is. The formula for the volume of a rectangular prism is

$$\text{volume} = \text{length} \cdot \text{width} \cdot \text{height}$$

but *volume* itself is a measure of the amount of three-dimensional stuff that an object can hold.

Suppose I have a box with dimensions $2 \cdot 3 \cdot 4$ inches. The volume of the box is $2 \cdot 3 \cdot 4 = 24$ cubic inches, right? So if I fill the box with rice, I have 24 cubic inches of rice.

Now, suppose I have a cylindrical bowl that is just large enough to hold that rice—that is, if I pour all the rice from the box into the bowl, the bowl is completely filled.

The box and the bowl hold exactly the same amount of three-dimensional stuff, whether it's rice, water, flour, sand, or just air. That's what it means for them to have the same volume.

It turns out that a gallon container can hold 231 cubic inches of stuff. This is independent of the shape of the container—whether it's a box, or a cylinder, or a sphere, or a truncated cone (like a disposable coffee cup, or some measuring cups), or a torus (i.e., a doughnut), or just some weird shape, like many perfume bottles. So any quart container will hold one-quarter of that amount, or $231 \div 4$ cubic inches of stuff; any pint container will hold half of $231 \div 4$, or $231 \div 8$ cubic inches of stuff; and any cup container will hold half of $231 \div 8$, or $231 \div 16$ cubic inches of stuff.

Different common shapes have different formulas that can be used to compute their volumes. In the example of the box and the bowl, suppose I know that the bowl is 6 inches high. I can use the formula for volume,

$$\text{volume} = \pi \cdot \text{radius}^2 \cdot \text{height}$$

to find out the radius of the bowl by solving for radius:

$$\text{radius} = \sqrt{\frac{\text{volume}}{\pi \cdot \text{height}}}$$

Or, if I know that the radius of the bowl is 4 inches, I can find out the height by solving for height:

$$\text{height} = \sqrt{\frac{\text{volume}}{\pi \cdot \text{radius}^2}}$$

But no matter what dimensions they have, if the box and the bowl can hold the same amount of stuff, they have the same volume. The next time you're in a cooking equipment store, take a look at the various measuring cups. They may all have different shapes, but a measuring cup marked "1 cup" will hold 231 ÷ 16 cubic inches of water, sugar, flour, or anything else you fill it with no matter what the shape of the cup.

So if you know how many cups of rice a box will hold, you already know the volume of the box, although you may want to convert it to different units, like cubic inches, or cubic centimeters, or liters, or whatever. It's sort of like this: suppose I tell you that the length of a certain room is exactly 16 times the length of a particular shoe box. If you have the shoe box, you can measure it in inches, or centimeters, or whatever other units you prefer; then you can multiply by 16 to get the length of the room. So if I tell you how many shoe boxes fit along one wall of the room, you know the length of the room and you just have to convert it to units that you like better.

—Dr. Math, The Math Forum

A Rectangular Prism

Dear Dr. Math,

I have been doing a geometry scavenger hunt for school, and I have been pondering this for days: is it possible to have a rectangular prism that has a volume greater than its surface area? I have tried everything I can think of, and I can't figure it out! If it is possible, could you please give me the measurements?

Yours truly,

Lorraine

Dear Lorraine,

As a matter of fact, it is possible if you only consider the numerical value of each, disregarding the units of measurement (because area is square and volume is cubic). Think about this: when you make a rectangular prism (a box) bigger and bigger, its surface area grows about as fast as the square of its lengths (the lengths of its edges), and its volume grows about as fast as the cube of its lengths.

So think about a really simple case: a cube. If the edge length is *s*, the surface area of a cube is $6s^2$, and the volume is s^3. Can you pick a value of *s* that makes s^3 bigger than $6s^2$? However you answer that, whether s^3 is larger or smaller than $6s^2$ will depend on the units you choose. (Remember the answer to "Can Area Be Larger Than Perimeter?" on page 54?)

—Dr. Math, The Math Forum

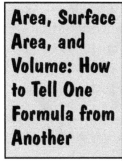

Area, Surface Area, and Volume: How to Tell One Formula from Another

Dear Dr. Math,

I am having trouble memorizing the geometric formulas. Say you have to calculate the volume of a can and you have the radius. How can you tell that you are right and that you haven't done the area?

Yours truly,

Leon

Dear Leon,

There's a nice simple answer to that last question, though it won't solve everything for you. Suppose you vaguely remember that one formula for a cylinder is $\pi r^2 h$ (pi times radius squared times height) and another is $2\pi rh$ (twice pi times the radius times the height). You can tell which is the area and which is the volume by looking at the dimensions.

Suppose the radius is 2 inches and the height is 3 inches, and we accept 3.14 for pi. Then our first formula gives

$$\pi r^2 h = 3.14 \cdot (2 \text{ in})^2 \cdot 3 \text{ in}$$
$$= 3.14 \cdot 4 \text{ in}^2 \cdot 3 \text{ in}$$
$$= 37.68 \text{ in}^3$$

Do you see how I work with the units just as if they were numbers (or variables in algebra) and end up with the units for the answer? Since the units in^3 are cubic, this is a volume.

Similarly, for the second formula

$$2\pi rh = 2 \cdot 3.14 \cdot 2 \text{ in} \cdot 3 \text{ in}$$
$$= 6.28 \cdot 6 \text{ in}^2$$
$$= 37.68 \text{ in}^2$$

we get square units, in^2, so this is an area.

In general, you can just count the dimensions in the formula. There are three dimensions represented in r^2h, so it's a three-dimensional quantity, a volume. There are only two dimensions represented in rh, so it's an area.

Finally, probably the best way to learn these formulas is to know where they come from. You're probably not ready to figure out the sphere formulas on your own, but the cylinder formulas are simple. The lateral surface area is just the circumference of the base circle ($2\pi r$) times the height (h)—picture how you'd make the side of a cylinder by rolling up a rectangle. The volume is the area of the base circle (πr^2) times the height (h)—just like the volume of a rectangular solid.

So how can you memorize the formulas? I would suggest you write all of the geometric formulas down in a table and look for relationships. I've just told you how the formulas for a circle and a rectangle combine to give you a cylinder. The more of those you can find, the better. You'll also find some less obvious ones: the volumes of a sphere and a cone have an interesting relationship. Make friends with the formulas, and they'll reveal some of their personal secrets to you.

—Dr. Math, The Math Forum

Nets of Solids

Imagine that you have a sheet of paper and you want to draw something so that when you cut it out and fold it, you can make a three-dimensional figure. The drawing that results in the solid figure is called a net. You'll usually need to add tabs to the edges of the figures if you actually want to glue them together, but you won't need tabs if you use tape to hold them together.

Dear Dr. Math,

In our geometry project, we are supposed to draw the net of various shapes. What is the net of a shape?

Yours truly,

Lorraine

Dear Lorraine,

The **net** of a polyhedron (a three-dimensional shape made up of flat faces) is a plane diagram that shows how the edges of the polyhedron are connected. Below shows you several nets in a geometrical sense: the shape is flattened out by cutting along the edges. You can cut these nets out and actually build the shape. You will often see tabs stuck to the sides of the net, which will make it easier to build a model from the net. Here's a chart:

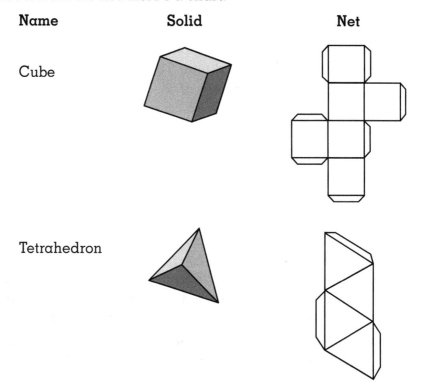

Name	Solid	Net
Cube		
Tetrahedron		

Name	Solid	Net
Octahedron		
Dodecahedron		
Icosahedron		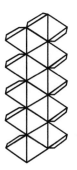

—Dr. Math, The Math Forum

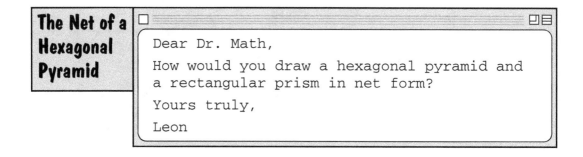

Dear Dr. Math,

How would you draw a hexagonal pyramid and a rectangular prism in net form?

Yours truly,

Leon

Dear Leon,

I believe the kind of net you are asking about is a flat drawing that can be folded into the shape you want. In both cases, you can start with the base (a hexagon or a rectangle), then add the sides, folded down flat; and finally, for the prism, attach the top to one of the sides. Here are my attempts at both, to suggest how it should look.

Hexagonal pyramid: fold all six points up so that they meet:

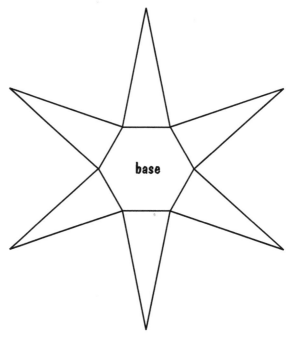

(All twelve edges of the side faces must be the same length for a regular pyramid.)

Rectangular prism: fold the four sides up, then fold the top over:

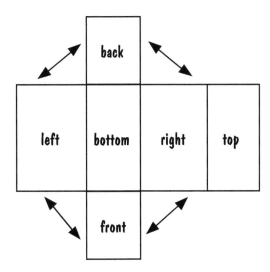

Pay attention to which edges have to have the same length so that when they are folded they will meet properly. For example, there are eight edges whose length is the height of the box (marked with arrows in the diagram).

—*Dr. Math, The Math Forum*

Resources on the Web

Learn more about three-dimensional geometric figures at these Math Forum sites:

Math Forum: Crystals

mathforum.org/alejandre/workshops/toc.crystal.html
Students studying polyhedra enjoy seeing the structures as they occur in the real world. Crystalline structures can be categorized

into seven crystal systems. Students can access links to photographs of beautiful crystals. Paper models of crystals can be made by printing out nets of crystals and constructing the models. CrystalMaker software gives students experience with ball-and-stick, space-filling, wire-frame, stick, dot surface cloud, and polyhedral models of crystals.

Math Forum: Polyhedra in the Classroom

mathforum.org/alejandre/workshops/unit14.html

Middle school student activities to pursue with a computer in the classroom. Introduction to polyhedra; paper nets to print out and fold; Kaleidotile; buckyballs; crystals (paper nets, systems); cube coloring problems; and links to polyhedra on the Web.

Math Forum: Studying Polyhedra

mathforum.org/alejandre/applet.polyhedra.html

What is a polyhedron? A definition and a Java applet will help in exploring the five regular polyhedra to find how many faces and vertices each has, and what polygons make up the faces.

Shodor Organization: Project Interactivate: Surface Area and Volume

shodor.org/interactivate/activities/sa_volume

This activity allows the user to manipulate polyhedra to experiment with surface area and volume.

Utah State University: National Library of Virtual Manipulatives: Platonic Solids

matti.usu.edu/nlvm2/nav/frames_asid_128_g_3_t_3.html

This virtual manipulative allows students to display, rotate, and resize Platonic solids. It also allows them to select vertices, edges, and faces, and to show that the number of vertices minus the number of edges plus the number of faces is equal to 2 (Euler's formula).

Utah State University: National Library of Virtual Manipulatives: Platonic Solids Duals

matti.usu.edu/nlvm2/nav/frames_asid_131_g_3_t_3.html

With this applet it can be seen that a Platonic dual is two Platonic solids: one placed inside the other. The vertices of the inner Platonic solid are the center points of each of the surfaces of the outer Platonic solid.

Utah State University: National Library of Virtual Manipulatives: Platonic Solids—Slicing

matti.usu.edu/nlvm2/nav/frames_asid_126_g_3_t_3.html

This virtual manipulative displays a Platonic solid on the left and the outline of a plane that slices through it on the right.

Utah State University: National Library of Virtual Manipulatives: Space Blocks

matti.usu.edu/nlvm2/nav/frames_asid_195_g_3_t_2.html

Create and discover patterns using three-dimensional blocks.

PART 5

Symmetry

Symmetries create patterns that help us organize our world conceptually. Symmetric patterns occur in nature and are invented by artists, craftspeople, musicians, choreographers, and mathematicians.

Symmetry is a topic very close to all of us because we carry examples of it wherever we go! Hold your hands out, palms down with your thumbs touching. Do they look something like this?

This is an example of reflectional symmetry. Reflection is one type of **rigid motion**—that is, a movement that preserves shape or keeps it looking the same. (Rigid motions are also called rigid trans-formations, or isometries.) When you flip a handprint over to make an image with reflectional symmetry, it doesn't change the shape of the handprint into any other shape. Each type of symmetry in the plane results from a different type of rigid motion, and we'll talk about them all in this section.

In this part, Dr. Math explains

- rigid motions: rotation, reflection, translation, and glide reflection
- symmetries
- lines of symmetry
- tessellations

Rigid Motions: Rotation, Reflection, Translation, and Glide Reflection

Rigid motions involve moving things around the plane so that their relative measurements remain the same. Once you rotate a square, for example, all the side lengths, the diagonals, and the angles still have their original measurements. This section will introduce you to the various types of rigid motions in the plane: rotation, reflection, translation, and glide reflection.

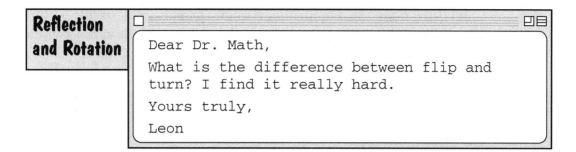

Dear Dr. Math,

What is the difference between flip and turn? I find it really hard.

Yours truly,

Leon

Dear Leon,

Flip and turn are meant to be kid-friendly replacements for the technical terms "reflection" and "rotation." You're supposed to be able to picture them more easily using the simpler words. So let's relate their math meaning to their everyday use.

If I *turn* around, I pivot so that I face a different direction. Here I'll turn, or rotate, a square by about 45 degrees:

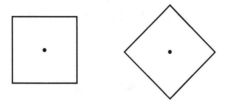

A **rotation** doesn't change the shape, but it will change the position of parts of the shape and the direction it faces. It's best to picture rotation as rotation in place—that is, imagine my first square as a piece of paper, put a pin through the middle, and rotate it around the pin so that the center of my second figure is actually in the same place as the center of the first.

The point of rotation can be in different places:

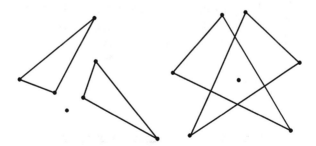

If I *flip* a pancake, I'm turning it over. The same sort of thing happens if I look at myself in a mirror; the left and right sides switch places. Here I'll flip a right triangle over:

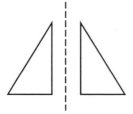

Notice that I can't make this same change by turning; if the triangle were a separate piece of paper, I would have had to turn it over. If I had to keep the same side on top, I would have had to replace it with a new copy made backward; or I could have just put a mirror along the dotted line and only seen the **reflection** of the original triangle in the new position. You can also imagine turning (flipping) a page in a book; the dotted line is then the middle of the book. Again, the line can be in different places. These are both reflections:

—*Dr. Math, The Math Forum*

Reflection and Rotation

Dear Dr. Math,

Can rotation of a figure and reflection of that same figure yield the same result at times? If a shape with one line of symmetry is reflected across a line, this same image could be obtained by rotating the shape, right?

Yours truly,

Lorraine

Dear Lorraine,

I think you are talking about something like this:

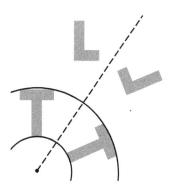

Here I drew a T and an L and reflected both across a line. The image of the L clearly can be obtained only by reflection; but the T image can also be obtained by rotation about a point on the line, as shown.

So if a problem asks for any transformation that will take the first T into the other, you can use either the reflection or the rotation. Of course, if the corresponding points on the original and the image were marked, that would force you to choose either the reflection or the rotation.

Here's a pair of T's, the second of which could only be obtained by rotation:

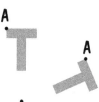

And here's a pair that used reflection:

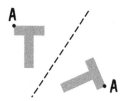

Do you see how we can tell which pair used which motion?

—*Dr. Math, The Math Forum*

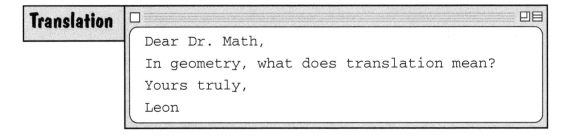

Dear Dr. Math,

In geometry, what does translation mean?

Yours truly,

Leon

Dear Leon,

It means to move from one place to another. To translate an object means to move it without rotating or reflecting it. Every **translation** has a direction and a distance. That's all it needs—it's the simplest kind of rigid motion. It gets combined with another rigid motion, reflection, to make yet another type of rigid motion called a glide reflection. Here are some translations. The arrows indicate direction and distance:

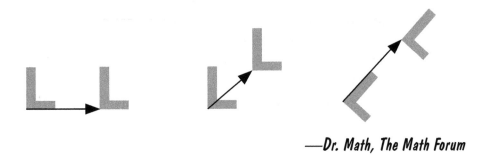

—*Dr. Math, The Math Forum*

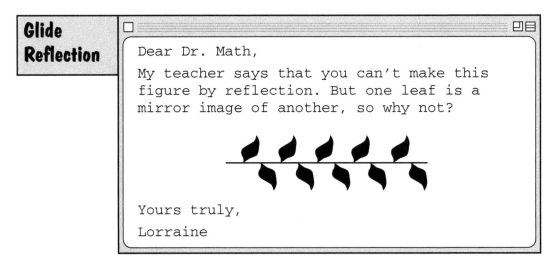

Dear Dr. Math,

My teacher says that you can't make this figure by reflection. But one leaf is a mirror image of another, so why not?

Yours truly,

Lorraine

Dear Lorraine,

If you reflected a leaf on the top, you'd get a leaf on the bottom directly beneath the original leaf. But in this figure, the bottom leaves are offset—they've been moved along the line a little, away from the matching leaves. So you have to reflect a leaf, then move it along the line. That's a **glide reflection.** You could also glide the leaf along the line, then reflect it—the effect is the same. Here's another example, with the reflection line and the translation marked. Can you see where the other R would be if we did the reflection and translation in the other order?

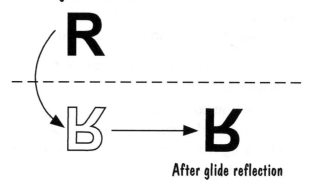

Before glide reflection

After glide reflection

—*Dr. Math, The Math Forum*

Symmetries

Now we know about rigid motions. How do they relate to symmetry? **Symmetry** comes from a Greek word meaning "having the same measure." Different parts of a symmetric figure have the same measure, the same proportions. That should sound familiar—rigid motions preserve the measures of shapes. And sure enough, the four different rigid motions are what you have to do to get the four different types of symmetry in the plane.

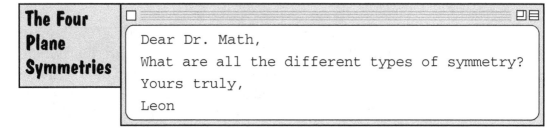

```
Dear Dr. Math,
What are all the different types of symmetry?
Yours truly,
Leon
```

Dear Leon,

Plane symmetries are derived from rigid motions, or transformations. That means you move all the points that make up a figure around the plane so that their positions relative to one another remain the same, although their absolute positions may change. In other words, the figure looks the same when it's been transformed. There are four types of rigid motion in the plane and thus four types of plane symmetry:

1. Rotation of a figure can make a symmetry called rotational symmetry.
2. Reflection can make another type called reflectional symmetry. This is also known as mirror symmetry, bilateral (from "bi" meaning "two" and "lateral" meaning "side") symmetry, or line symmetry.
3. Translating an object can result in translational symmetry.
4. The fourth type of symmetry is glide reflectional symmetry. I bet you can guess what rigid motion this comes from!

Not every rigid motion results in a symmetric figure. Picture a table knife. Imagine rotating it 90 degrees clockwise around a point at the base of the handle. What does it look like?

Now you have two knives at right angles to each other. Does the figure have rotational symmetry? No, it does not. Imagine rotating both knives—the whole

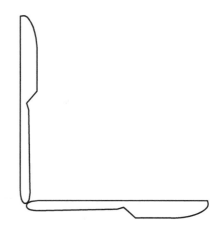

figure—by 90 degrees. What do you get? A pair of knives pointing east and south instead of north and east. Does that figure look the same as the original?

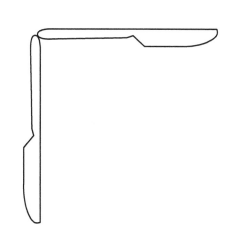

No, you can tell which is which. To get an image with rotational symmetry, you'd have to duplicate the knife two more times—at 180 degrees and 270 degrees—so that the knives formed an addition sign. That would be a figure you could rotate as a whole, and have it look the same.

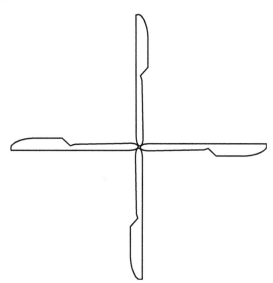

A figure has rotational symmetry if you can rotate it around a point so that its rotated image coincides with the original figure after turning it less than 360 degrees. A special kind of rotational symmetry is called point symmetry, which occurs when the figure has 180-degree rotational symmetry. If you picture an S with a point in the middle, then rotate it around that point by 180 degrees, you'll see the same S. That's point symmetry.

A figure has reflectional symmetry if you flip the figure over a line so that the resulting image coincides with the original. There are other names for reflectional symmetry, including line symmetry, bilateral symmetry (because the line of symmetry divides the object into two ["bi"] sides ["lateral"] that look like each other), and mirror symmetry (because you can place a mirror on the line of symmetry to see the symmetry).

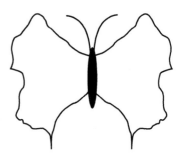

Translational symmetry is a bit more involved. You remember that a translation is the simplest of the rigid transformations, just sliding a shape along a line to another place. Well, translational symmetry is when you have a bunch of shapes translated along a single line. It's not translational symmetry if you only take part of a pattern. Here's an example of what I mean:

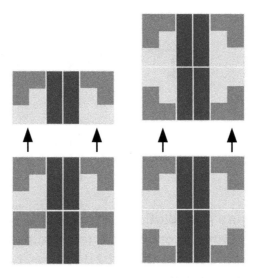

Because the figure on the left is made up of two units that are identical by translation, you can repeat the unit to translate it. The figure on the right, though, is made up of two reflected units. To maintain the translational symmetry, you have to use the whole thing. If you only used the top half of it, you would break the pattern. And the pattern has to go on forever for it to be translational symmetry. (You don't have to draw forever, though—mathematicians just assume the pattern continues.)

Glide reflectional symmetry is the only type of symmetry that involves more than one step because glide reflection is the only rigid motion that involves two steps. And because glide reflectional symmetry involves translation, it shares a property with translational symmetry that a pattern must be considered infinite. Let me put that in concrete terms: remember that leafy vine? It's got glide reflectional symmetry if we consider it to be an infinite pattern.

(One sneaky way to make a design that has translational or glide reflectional symmetry without having to make it infinite is to expand it into three dimensions: if you put a repeating pattern around the rim of a bowl, it will go around in a circle forever!)

—Dr. Math, The Math Forum

Lines of Symmetry

Reflectional symmetry is one of the easiest symmetries to spot, once you've trained yourself to see the lines of symmetry. What's a **line of symmetry**? It's where the mirror goes in a mirror-symmetric picture. Here's an example. Your right hand by itself is not symmetric, but your two hands held up next to each other are symmetric. We can tell because if we put a mirror on the line between them and looked at the mirror image of one hand next to itself, it would look just like the two hands together. Or if you put your handprints on a piece of paper and folded the paper in half on the line of symmetry between them, you could hold the paper up to the light and see only one handprint, because they would line up on top of each other. The fold is a line of symmetry.

Horizontal and Vertical Symmetry

Dear Dr. Math,

I have a project where I have to look for things outside that involve symmetry. One of the things I have to find is an example of horizontal symmetry, and I have no idea what that is. I tried to look it up in a dictionary, but it is just not making any sense. Can you please help me?

Yours truly,

Lorraine

Dear Lorraine,

Horizontal and vertical symmetry are reflectional, or mirror, symmetries, with the mirror lined up in particular directions. Let's take some simple examples:

Vertical symmetry: if you draw a vertical line down the middle of an object with vertical symmetry, the two sides will be mirror images of each other.

Examples of capital letters that have vertical symmetry are

A H I M O T U V W X Y

Horizontal symmetry: if you draw a horizontal line across the middle of an object with horizontal symmetry, the top will be a mirror image of the bottom.

-----B------

Examples of capital letters that have horizontal symmetry are

B C D E H I O X

Words with horizontal symmetry include

BIDED, DECIDED, BOXED,
OXIDE, HIDE, CHOICE

This drawing of a bow and arrow is a nice example of horizontal symmetry:

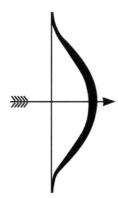

Some flags have horizontal symmetry; here are a few of them:

Austria's flag is three horizontal stripes of red, white, and red.

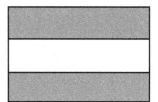

The flag of the Bahamas has a black triangle on the left with three horizontal stripes of turquoise, yellow, and turquoise.

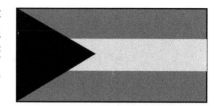

The left side of the Bahrain flag is white and the right side is red with a zigzag pattern joining the two.

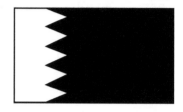

Now see what other examples you can find on your own.

—*Dr. Math, The Math Forum*

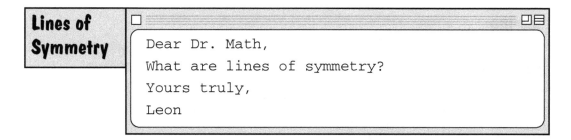

Dear Dr. Math,
What are lines of symmetry?
Yours truly,
Leon

Dear Leon,

A line of symmetry is an imaginary line drawn through a plane figure; if the figure is flipped over using that line as an axis of rotation, you get the same figure back again.

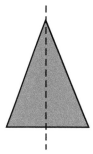

We can create a simple example with an isosceles triangle. Suppose that you orient the figure so that the odd side (length not equal to the other two, which are equal to each other) is horizontal, and the opposite vertex is above it. Then the line of symmetry is the altitude from that vertex down to that odd side. It is not part of the original figure, which is why I called it imaginary, but it is easy to construct.

If you flip the triangle over using this altitude as a line of symmetry, the equal sides will be swapped, the equal base angles will be swapped, the vertex angle will be left alone, and the base will be left in place. You will get an identical copy of the original figure.

Another, more complicated example is a square. There are four lines of symmetry. Two are the diagonals of the square, and two go through the middles of the sides. Can you see why? These lines are not part of the original figure but are constructed from it.

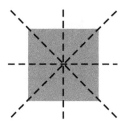

—*Dr. Math, The Math Forum*

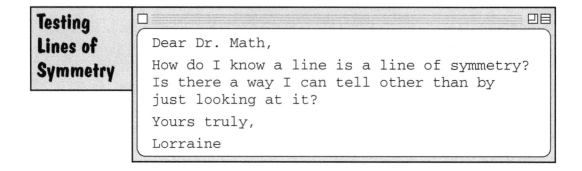

Dear Dr. Math,

How do I know a line is a line of symmetry? Is there a way I can tell other than by just looking at it?

Yours truly,

Lorraine

Dear Lorraine,

You can test a line to see if it's a line of symmetry for a given shape by reflecting a point that's on the shape over the line. If the point's reflection is another point on the shape, the line may be a line of symmetry.

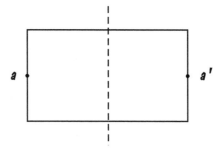

If the point's reflection lands somewhere not on the shape, the line is definitely not a line of symmetry.

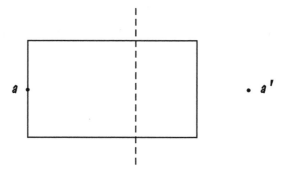

Here's why you have to test points from different parts of the shape:

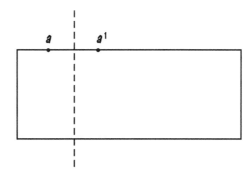

This is *not* a line of symmetry! Generally if you test the vertices of a figure made of straight line segments, and they agree with each other, then you can be sure that you have a line of symmetry.

So we can define symmetry about a line of reflection this way: if we reflect every point on the shape over the line, we end up with another point on the same shape every time.

—*Dr. Math, The Math Forum*

Lines of Symmetry in a Circle

Dear Dr. Math,

How many lines of symmetry are there in a circle? This has been an ongoing conversation in our class. We've asked many teachers, and we have come up with three answers: 180, 360, and infinitely many. Which one is correct?

Sincerely,

Leon

Dear Leon,

It seems you are asking the question: how many lines can a circle be reflected about and still be self-coincident (i.e., fall back onto itself)?

The answer is infinitely many. Take any diameter of the circle and reflect the circle about that diameter, and it will be self-coincident. Those of you who thought of 180 and 360 were probably thinking of the number of degrees in a circle—but not only is there a line of symmetry at each degree, there's one at each half of a degree, at each eighth of a degree, at each seventeenth of a degree . . .

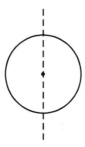

There are an infinite number of diameters of a circle, so there are an infinite number of such lines.

Notice that the circle is also self-coincident under any rotation. So there are an infinite number of symmetry rotations of the circle.

—Dr. Math, The Math Forum

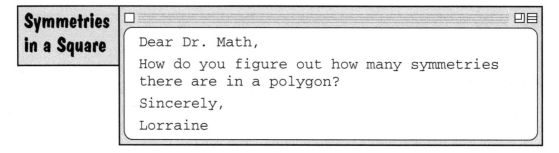

Symmetries in a Square

Dear Dr. Math,

How do you figure out how many symmetries there are in a polygon?

Sincerely,

Lorraine

Dear Lorraine,

Let's take a square as a good starting point. Single polygons do not have translational or glide reflectional symmetry, so all we have to worry about is reflectional and rotational symmetries.

Number the corners of a square like this:

When we flip the square about a line of symmetry or rotate the square, we will call this a rigid motion, because the square maintains its shape (i.e., it doesn't get squashed or anything). A square has four lines of symmetry: the horizontal line, the vertical line, and the two diagonals. It also has four rotations: the 90-degree turn, the 180-degree turn, the 270-degree turn, and the 360-degree turn.

The horizontal line flip switches 1 and 3 and switches 2 and 4.

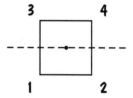

The vertical line flip switches 1 and 2 and switches 3 and 4.

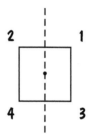

The 1,4-diagonal line flip switches 3 and 2 and leaves both 1 and 4 fixed.

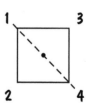

The 3,2-diagonal line flip switches 1 and 4 and leaves both 3 and 2 fixed.

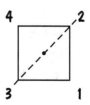

The 360-degree (or 0-degree, however you look at it) rotation leaves everything fixed.

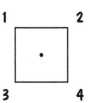

The 90-degree rotation moves 1 to 2, 2 to 4, 4 to 3, and 3 to 1.

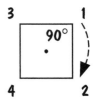

The 180-degree rotation moves 1 to 4 and 2 to 3.

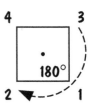

The 270-degree rotation moves 1 to 3, 3 to 4, 4 to 2, and 2 to 1.

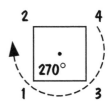

Note that any one of the rigid motions followed by another rigid motion gives us a different rigid motion. For example, the horizontal flip, followed by the 90-degree rotation, switches 3 and 2 and leaves 1 and 4 fixed, which is the same as the 1,4-diagonal flip.

— *Dr. Math, The Math Forum*

Tessellation

Have you ever stared at a bathroom floor to figure out the pattern in the tiles? A flat-plane pattern is called a **tiling** or a **tessellation.** Any regular pattern that tiles the plane (which means it covers the plane with no gaps) is a tessellation. The first tessellations with actual tiles were done with square shapes, like this:

But there are many other possible patterns, as you'll see in this section.

As with translational and glide reflectional symmetries, tessellations are assumed to be infinite patterns. You don't really have to draw forever; you just have to have a pattern that *could* go on forever.

What Is a Tessellation?

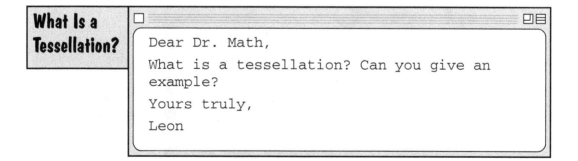

Dear Dr. Math,

What is a tessellation? Can you give an example?

Yours truly,

Leon

Dear Leon,

A dictionary will tell you that the word "tessellate" means to form or arrange small pieces (like squares) in a checkered or mosaic pattern. It is derived from the Ionic version of the Greek word "tesseres," which in English means "four."

The tessellation you might learn in middle school mathematics is a tiling of the plane using a square, a triangle, or a hexagon, where the geometric figures fit together without leaving any spaces. Imagine that you have a room in your house that you'd like to outfit with a new floor. You want to completely cover the floor with tile so that it looks nice. You don't want any gaps or holes showing between the tiles. Let's also say for this example that you can only have one shape of tile. You can use as many tiles as you need so that the whole floor is covered, but every tile has to be perfectly identical to every other tile in a regular tessellation.

If you can completely cover the floor with a certain shape of tile, we say that this shape tessellates the floor. With some shapes, you'll be able to cover the floor, and with others, you won't. If you try using a regular hexagon, for example, you'll succeed. This is because each hexagon snuggles nicely beside the others, with no gaps in between. We call that a regular tessellation. But if you try to use an octagon, you'll fail. Octagons do not snuggle nicely. If you combine octagons and squares, however, you can create a tessellation. The combination of more than one shape makes a semiregular tessellation.

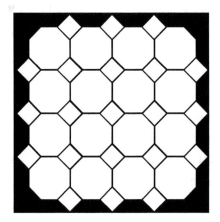

A semiregular tessellation of octagons and squares

—Dr. Math, The Math Forum

Dear Dr. Math,

I am looking for the proof of the statement that only three regular polygons tessellate in the Euclidean plane. I have an idea how it is done but am not quite sure how to write out the proof in a concise manner for a paper I am doing on tessellations. I would appreciate any information on this matter.

Yours truly,

Lorraine

Dear Lorraine,

A regular polygon has three or more sides and angles, all equal. For each of these, you can work out the interior measure of the angles. For a triangle, it's 60 degrees; for a square, it's 90 degrees; for a pentagon, it's 108 degrees; for a hexagon, it's 120 degrees; and for anything with more than six sides, it's more than 120 degrees.

Since the regular polygons in a tessellation must fill the plane at each vertex, the interior angle must be an exact divisor of 360 degrees. This works for the triangle, the square, and the hexagon, and you can show working tessellations for these figures.

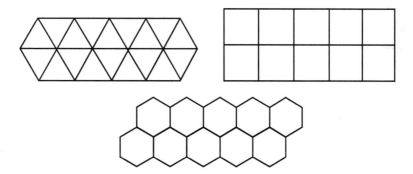

For all the others, the interior angles are not exact divisors of 360 degrees, and therefore those figures cannot tile the plane.

—Dr. Math, The Math Forum

Make a Tessellation

Dear Dr. Math,

Is it possible to make a tessellation with glide reflection, rotation, and translation all in one object?

Yours truly,

Leon

Dear Leon,

Yes, you can have tessellations that include three types of symmetries or even all four types (reflection, rotation, translation, glide reflection). There are two main ideas in the reason why:

1. In a symmetric pattern, if you have two symmetries, then you have the combination (also called composition or product) of the symmetries. For example, if your pattern has symmetries of rotation by 45 degrees and rotation by 90 degrees, then it also has rotation by 45 + 90 = 135 degrees. This pattern would also have rotation by 45, 90, 135, 180, 225, 270, 315, and 0 degrees.

2. All four types of symmetry can be made by combining reflections.
   - A rotation is the composition of two reflections in intersecting lines.
   - A translation is the composition of two reflections in parallel lines.
   - A glide reflection is the composition of a translation and a reflection, so it is the composition of three reflections.

—Dr. Math, The Math Forum

esources on the Web

Learn more about symmetry at these Math Forum sites:

Regular Tessellations

mathforum.org/pubs/boxer/tess.html

A middle school lesson utilizing BoxerMath.com's Tessellation Tool Java applet to help students understand why equilateral triangles, squares, and regular hexagons tessellate regularly in the Euclidean plane.

Repeated Reflections of an "R"

mathforum.org/sum95/suzanne/rex.html

Students draw a design with reflectional symmetry and rotational symmetry.

Sonya's Symmetry (English version)
Simetría de Sonya (Spanish version)

mathforum.org/alejandre/mathfair/sonya.html

mathforum.org/alejandre/mathfair/sonyaspanish.html

In this activity from Frisbie Middle School's Multicultural Math Fair, students use a manipulative to see and draw reflections.

Pre-Algebra Problem of the Week: Symmetry Surprise

mathforum.org/prealgpow/solutions/solution.ehtml?puzzle=219

Identify the types of symmetries in each of three patterns.

Tessellation Tutorials

mathforum.org/sum95/suzanne/tess.intro.html

A series of tutorials that teach students how to tessellate (somewhat in the style of the art of M. C. Escher) using HyperCard for black and white and/or HyperStudio for color, ClarisWorks, LogoWriter, templates, or simple straightedge and compass.

Middle School Problem of the Week: Tiling Triangles

mathforum.org/midpow/solutions/solution.ehtml?puzzle=143

Given the dimensions of a large triangle, find the dimensions of the twenty-five small triangles that tile it.

Types of Symmetry in the Plane

mathforum.org/sum95/suzanne/symsusan.html

Rotation, translation, reflection, and glide reflection, with illustrations and problems for consideration.

Using Kali (English version)
Usando Kali (Spanish version)

mathforum.org/alejandre/mathfair/kali.html

mathforum.org/alejandre/mathfair/kalispanish.html

In this activity from Frisbie Middle School's Multicultural Math Fair, students use an interactive two-dimensional Euclidean symmetry pattern editor.

Appendix: Geometric Figures..........

Some handy formulas for calculating area, perimeter, volume, and surface area.

Abbreviations

A: area

P: perimeter

V: volume

S: surface area

b: base

B: area of the base

s: side

h: height

l: length

w: width

d: diameter

C: circumference

r: radius

f: number of faces

e: number of edges

v: number of vertices

Triangle Formulas

$$A = \frac{1}{2} \cdot b \cdot h$$
$$P = s_1 + s_2 + s_3$$

Types of Triangles

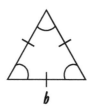

Equilateral Triangle

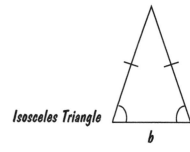

Isosceles Triangle

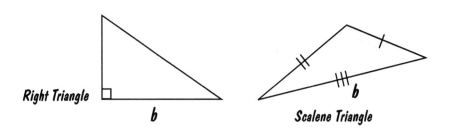

Right Triangle

Scalene Triangle

b

b

Quadrilaterals

General Quadrilateral
$P = s_1 + s_2 + s_3 + s_4$
(angles add up to 360°)

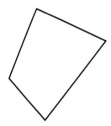

Square
$A = s^2$
$P = 4s$

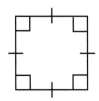

Rectangle
$A = l \cdot w$
$P = 2l + 2w$

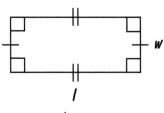

w

l

Parallelogram
$A = b \cdot h$ (Not s, not w!)
$P = 2s_1 + 2s_2$

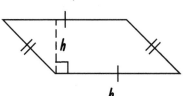

h

b

Rhombus
$A = b \cdot h$ (Not s, not w!)
$P = 4s$

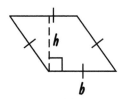

h

b

Trapezoid

$$A = h \cdot \frac{b_1 + b_2}{2}$$

$P = b_1 + b_2 + s_1 + s_2$

$P = b_1 + b_2 + 2s$ if trapezoid is isosceles

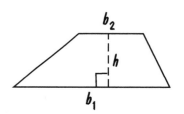

Kite

$$A = \frac{diagonal_1 \cdot diagonal_2}{2}$$

$P = 2s_1 + 2s_2$

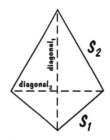

Regular Polygons

Triangle

Square

Pentagon

Hexagon

Octagon

Circle

$A = \pi r^2$

$P = \pi d$

Rectangular Prism or Cuboid

$V = l \cdot w \cdot h$

$S = 2lw + 2wh + 2hl$

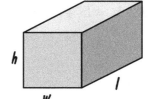

Cube

$V = s^3$

$S = 6s^2$

Prism

$V = Bh$

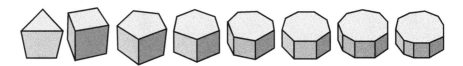

$S = 2B + \text{perimeter of base} \cdot h$

Pyramid

$V = \dfrac{1}{3} \cdot Bh$

$S = \dfrac{\text{slant height} \cdot \text{perimeter of base}}{2} + \text{area of base}$

(for regular pyramids)

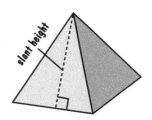

Regular Polyhedra

Euler's formula: $f - e + v = 2$

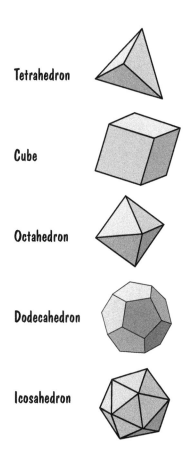

Tetrahedron

Cube

Octahedron

Dodecahedron

Icosahedron

Other Solids

Cylinder

Right Circular Cylinder

h = length of lateral edge

$V = Bh$

lateral surface area $= 2\pi r \cdot h = \pi d \cdot h$

$S = \pi d(r + h) = 2 \cdot B + (\pi d \cdot h)$

Cone

$$V = \frac{1}{3} \cdot Bh$$

Right Circular Cone

$$\text{slant height} = \sqrt{r^2 + h^2}$$

$$\text{lateral surface area} = \pi r \cdot \text{slant height}$$

$$S = \pi r(r + \text{slant height})$$

$$V = \frac{1}{3} \cdot \pi r^2 \cdot h$$

Sphere

$$s = 4\pi r^2 = \pi d^2$$

$$V = \frac{4\pi}{3} \cdot r^3 = \frac{\pi}{6} d^3$$

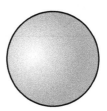

Glossary..

acute angle An angle measuring less than 90 degrees.

alternate angle When two parallel lines are crossed by a transversal line, alternate angles are the ones on either the inside or the outside of the parallel lines (not both), one from the group of angles around each parallel line, and on opposite sides of the transversal from each other.

angle The joint or bend between two intersecting lines, line segments, or rays in the plane; in three dimensions, the bend between two intersecting planes.

area The portion of the plane enclosed by a figure in the plane. See also **surface area.**

base A side or face considered as the bottom part, or foundation, of a geometric figure. In an isosceles triangle, the side that is not a leg, or is not equal in length to another side; in a quadrilateral, the side you consider as the flat-on-the-ground side for the purposes of measurement; in three dimensions, any side of a figure designated as such, often one that is flat on the ground from the viewer's perspective.

Cartesian geometry The study of geometric forms in the coordinate plane. Named for René Descartes, who was instrumental in developing the coordinate plane.

chord A line segment whose endpoints are points on a circle. A diameter is a chord that passes through the center of the circle.

circle The set of all points in a plane that are a given distance from a given point.

circumference The distance around the edge of a circle.

complement An angle that is paired with another angle so that the sum of their measures is 90 degrees.

congruent Having the same dimensions. If you put congruent shapes on transparent paper and hold them up on top of each other, you can't tell them apart.

coordinate plane The grid system in which the x-axis (horizontal) and the y-axis (vertical) provide reference points; coordinates tell you locations in the plane and are determined by the distance along the axes.

corresponding angle When two parallel lines are crossed by a transversal line, the corresponding angles are in the same location around the two parallel lines relative to the transversal. In other words, if the parallel lines are horizontal, the top left angle around the top parallel line corresponds with the top left angle around the bottom parallel line. Corresponding angles have the same measure.

degree A unit of measure of angles; there are 360 degrees (written 360°) in the circle.

diameter The distance across the widest part of a circle; twice the radius. Also, a chord that passes through the center of the circle.

edge A line segment at the boundary of a polygon; a line segment at the intersection of two faces of a polyhedron.

equilateral triangle A triangle in which all the sides are congruent and all the angles are congruent.

expression A symbol, number, or combination of either or both, representing a quantity or relation between quantities. If an equation is a mathematical sentence, an expression is a mathematical phrase.

exterior The outside of something; exterior walls are the outsides of buildings.

glide reflection A rigid motion combining translation and reflection. A symmetric pattern produced by a glide reflection must be presumed to be infinite.

gradient A measure of angles; there are 400 gradients in a circle.

horizontal Parallel to the horizon; oriented side to side rather than up and down (i.e., the orientation of the x-axis).

hypotenuse The side opposite the right angle in a right triangle.

interior The inside of something; interior walls don't show from the outsides of buildings.

isosceles triangle A triangle having two sides, called the legs, of equal length.

kite A quadrilateral with two pairs of adjacent sides with equal lengths. (The other common definition, though not used in this book, says that the two pairs must have different lengths, meaning that a rhombus and a square are not special cases of a kite.)

legs The sides of an isosceles triangle that have equal length, or the sides of a right triangle that are adjacent to the right angle. Also the (usually) nonparallel sides of a trapezoid.

line One of the three undefined figures in geometry, a line has no thickness, is perfectly straight, and goes on forever in both directions. Two points determine a unique line.

line of symmetry A line over which a figure can be reflected, resulting in a figure that looks exactly like the original.

line segment A finite portion of a line, often denoted by its endpoints.

net A two-dimensional representation of a three-dimensional shape; a net shows all the faces of a given three-dimensional figure laid out in two dimensions, so if the two-dimensional shape were cut out of paper and folded along the joins, it would make the three-dimensional shape.

obtuse angle An angle measuring between 90 and 180 degrees.

one-dimensional An object that has a measurement in only one direction. A line is one-dimensional.

origin The point in the Cartesian coordinate system at which the x- and y-axes cross.

parallel Lines in the same plane that have the same slope and thus never meet are considered parallel, as are line segments that would never meet if extended into lines. Planes, or shapes within two planes, are parallel if they are the same distance apart everywhere on the shape or plane.

parallelogram   A quadrilateral with both pairs of opposite sides parallel.

perimeter   The distance around the sides of a polygon or a circle.

perpendicular   Lines or line segments that meet at right angles to each other.

pi   A constant, approximately equal to 3.1416, defined as the ratio of a circle's circumference to its diameter.

planar   Two-dimensional, or lying in a plane.

plane   One of the three undefined figures in geometry, a plane is a flat expanse, like a sheet of paper, that goes on forever. Any three points not on the same line, or a line and a point, determine a unique plane.

point   One of the three undefined figures in geometry, a point is a location with no length, width, or height.

polygon   A two-dimensional closed figure made up of straight line segments.

polyhedron (plural: **polyhedra**)   A three-dimensional closed figure made up of faces that are all polygons.

prism   A polyhedron with identical, parallel top and bottom faces connected by sides that are all parallelograms. In right prisms, the side faces are rectangles, meaning they meet the top and bottom faces at right angles.

protractor   An instrument for measuring angles on paper.

Pythagorean theorem   In a right triangle, the sum of the squares of the legs is equal to the square of the hypotenuse.

quadrilateral   A polygon with four sides.

radian   A measurement of angles; there are approximately 6.2831853, or 2π, radians in a circle.

radius (plural: **radii**)   The distance from the center of a circle to any point on its edge; half the diameter. Also, a segment whose endpoints are the center of the circle and a point anywhere on the circle.

ray   A portion of a line extending in one direction from a point; sometimes called a half line.

rectangle   A quadrilateral in which all the angles have the same measure (90 degrees).

reflection   A rigid motion in which a shape is reflected over a line, as it would be reflected if a mirror were held along the reflecting line.

reflex angle   An angle measuring more than 180 degrees.

regular   Made up of identical parts; a regular polygon is one in which all sides have the same length and all the angles have the same measure.

rhombus   A quadrilateral in which all sides have the same length.

right angle   An angle measuring 90 degrees.

rigid motion   A motion of an object that preserves its original measurements. Also known as rigid transformation or isometry.

rotation   A rigid motion in which a figure is rotated around a given point (either on or off the figure) by a given angle.

scalene   A polygon is scalene if its sides are all different lengths.

semiregular polyhedron   A polyhedron made up of two or more different types of regular polygons arranged in the same sequence around each vertex.

solid   A closed, three-dimensional figure.

square   A quadrilateral in which all sides have the same length and all angles are right angles.

surface area   The sum of the areas of the faces of a polyhedron. See also **area.**

supplement   An angle that is paired with another angle so that the sum of their measures is 180 degrees.

symmetry   A property by which a figure looks the same after a given rigid motion as it did before.

tessellation   A covering of the plane, sometimes referred to as a tiling, referring to the way that tiles cover a floor.

three-dimensional   An object that has a measurement in three directions. A cube is three-dimensional, as are all polyhedra.

tiling   See **tessellation.**

translation A rigid motion in which a figure is moved a given distance in a given direction.

transversal A line that intersects two parallel lines.

trapezoid A quadrilateral with at least one pair of parallel sides. (The other common definition, not used in this book, says it must have *exactly* one pair of parallel sides.)

two-dimensional An object that has a measurement in two directions. A plane is two-dimensional, as are all figures on a plane (squares, rectangles, circles).

undefined terms "Point," "line," and "plane" are the three undefined terms of geometry, upon which all other definitions are ultimately based. We can describe them and state their properties, but we can't provide rigorous mathematical definitions.

variable A symbol that stands for an unknown quantity in a mathematical expression or equation.

vertex (plural: **vertices**) The point of intersection of two lines, line segments, or rays that makes up an angle in two dimensions; the point of intersection of three or more planes or planar faces in three dimensions.

vertical Upright or perpendicular to the horizon. Compare **horizontal.**

vertical angles Where two lines intersect, vertical angles are those that are on opposite sides of the vertex from each other.

volume The three-dimensional space taken up by an object.

Index..

symmetry *(continued)*
  translational, 144, 146–147, 157
  vertical, 148–149

T

tessellation, 157–161
tetrahedra, 107, 108, 112, 114, 130
three-dimensional figures. *See also*
    polyhedra; solids; *specific figures*
  introduction to, 105–106
  resources on the Web, 133–135
tiling, 157–161
Timaeus (Plato), 112
translation, 138, 142, 143, 144, 146,
    160–161
translational symmetry, 144, 146–147,
    157
transversals, 18, 19, 20, 21, 40
trapezoids
  area of, 73, 78, 79–84
  base of, 76, 78
  defined, 44, 46
  height and length of, 76, 77–78, 79,
    82–84
  isosceles, 44, 46, 80–81
  in quadrilateral Venn diagram, 46
triangles
  area of, 66–67, 81
  base of, 32, 76
  in circles, 97
  congruent, 41
  equilateral, 32, 38
  height of, 76
  isosceles, 31, 32, 38
  legs of, 32
  lines of symmetry in, 151
  180 degrees in angles in, 39–40
  right, 34–39, 66–67, 81
  scalene, 31, 32–33
  special right, 37–39
  vertices in, 12

truncation, 115–117
two-dimensional geometric figures.
    See also specific figures
  areas and perimeters of, 49–52
  introduction to, 4–10
  measuring, 52
  resources on the Web, 47–48

U

undefined terms of geometry, 4–6
units of measurement. See measure-
    ment units

V

variables, 16
Venn diagram of quadrilaterals, 46
vertical angles, 22–24
vertical symmetry, 148–149
vertices, 11–12, 107, 108, 109, 111,
    113–114
volume
  of cylinders, 128–129
  defined, 122, 123
  measurement units for, 123, 125–127
  of rectangular prism, 124, 127–128
  surface area and, 123, 127–129

W

Web Sites
  area and perimeter, 84–85
  circles and pi, 104
  symmetry, 161–163
  three-dimensional figures, 133–135
  two-dimensional figures, 47–48
width, 53, 62–64, 75, 76

X

x-axis, 3, 7

Y

y-axis, 3, 7